59 Testimonies

$10.99

	DATE DUE	
2-6-97		
5-21-99		
4-22-00		
9-16-00		
6-5-01		
7-23-02		
11-21-02		
2-26-03		

CE National, Inc.
1003 Presidential Dr.
P. O. Box 365
Winona Lake, IN 46590

NFL PLAYERS TALK ABOUT FOOTBALL AND FAITH

FIRST & GOAL

DAVE BRANON

CE National, Inc.
1003 Presidential Dr.
P. O. Box 365
Winona Lake, IN 46590

MOODY PRESS
CHICAGO

CONTENTS

FOREWORD

By Joe Gibbs

When I retired as head coach of the Washington Redskins in 1992, I knew I'd be happy only if I kept doing something competitive. That's why making the transition from pacing the sidelines to pacing the pits was an easy one for me. Being an owner in auto racing fuels my competitive fire much like football once did.

As a coach, I had the thrill of winning three Super Bowls, and as a racecar owner, I've had the excitement of winning the NASCAR equivalent of the Super Bowl: the Daytona 500. In 1993, my second year as an owner, Dale Jarrett drove the Interstate Batteries Chevy into the winner's circle at Daytona.

There are some differences, though, between the two jobs. As the head coach of the Redskins, I would put in many sixteen- to twenty-hour days. Sometimes I would even camp out at the office, sleeping on a cot. Today, I'm dedicated to making sure Bobby Labonte has a good car and the crew has everything it needs to win, but I'm grateful those twenty-hour days are behind me.

So is my wife, Pat, and our sons, J. D. and Coy.

As difficult and as draining as it was to mold a bunch of football players into a winning unit, it was a job that I cherished. I still enjoy watching the game, and *First and Goal* brings back some of the memories. The NFL players profiled here talk about several important issues in their lives as athletes and representatives of Christ. Two that you will find in most of their stories are their love for the game and how humbling that game can be. It reminds them—and me—of who is ultimately in charge, the Lord of the Universe.

I still enjoy watching and analyzing this game. Being a head football coach was a dream come true for me. For whatever reason—and I truly think it is because God led me into the profession—I worked my way up to being a head coach. And along the way I learned some valuable lessons.

I started out as a volunteer assistant at San Diego State under Don Coryell and John Madden. Working under Madden, I learned how important it is when you make a taco run to Jack-in-the-Box that you get exactly what John Madden wants on his tacos. Seriously, much of what I know about coaching, I learned from Coryell and Madden.

Later I was named an assistant coach at Tampa Bay. There I learned a few things about communication. I had devised a scheme of hand signals for sending in plays from the sidelines. Problem was, our head coach, John McKay, was not comfortable with my newfangled approach. He preferred sending the plays in with a substitute. That sub would then relay the message to our quarterback, Doug Williams.

So, here I am on the sidelines, dictating a play to a receiver who's been clobbered in the head three times already. I'm telling him the play, "Trips right, zoom. Liz, 989. F-cross, snake." And he's supposed to run onto the field and tell Williams what I just said. You can imagine how well that would work.

Then it got worse. Coach McKay wanted me to go up in the booth, where I would relay the play by headset to a coach on the sideline, who would tell the groggy receiver, who would tell the quarterback. Needless to say, sometimes the play didn't come off as we designed it.

Another thing being a head coach taught me was humility. Finally, in 1981, I got that coveted head coaching job with the Washington Redskins. It didn't take long to find out that I didn't have much to be proud of. Before we could catch our breath, the Redskins were 0–5. In the nation's capital, to have your team be winless after five weeks is almost treasonous.

Eventually, we got things straightened out in Washington and went on to have some very good seasons. Yet I found out that even if we won most of the time, the job is humbling. In 1984, the second year we went to the Super Bowl, I was beginning to think I was pretty smart. Here I was, just a country boy from North Carolina—a PE major from San Diego State—and I had my team in the Super Bowl for the second year in a row.

But then everything went wrong. With 12 seconds to go in the first half, we were behind the Raiders 14–3, and I wanted to try to get some points back in a hurry. So even though we were on our own 12 yard line, I had Joe Theismann throwing on first down. His pass was intercepted by Jack Squirek, who ran it in for a touchdown. Instead of turning Theismann into the hero, I turned myself into the goat. We lost 38–9.

The next day the press labeled me a buffoon. I realized then that the only way you can please the world is to win every time.

All of these lessons mean so much more to me because I know who was teaching them to me. I know that God has my best interests at heart because I am a child of His. I have accepted Jesus Christ as my Savior, which makes me one of His children. I know that He wants to teach me about communication so I can convey to others the gospel. I know that He wants to teach me about humility so I will always be ready to serve Him.

I look back and I see how little I could control as a coach. Balls bounce different ways, players get hurt, and I realized the whole time how dependent I was on the Lord. In my years as a head coach, I was excited to discover others who shared my love for Jesus Christ and a dependence on Him.

I had guys on my team, such as Tim Johnson, Art Monk, and Darrell Green, who stood up for the Lord. And I respected players on opposing teams—guys like Reggie White and Frank Reich and Howard Cross—who depended on Jesus Christ.

That's why a book like *First and Goal* is so important today. It reveals what lessons God is teaching the men He is still using in the game to introduce others to His Son. Although I have left the game as a coach, my heart is still in it.

And my heart is still cheering for those men who keep God *first* and who make it their *goal* to serve Him.

First and goal. It's a great position to be in on the football field, but an even better position to be in when we contemplate our relationship to God. Read this book and learn how big NFL linemen, lanky quarterbacks, and small kickers have found the rewards of making God first in their lives.

JOE GIBBS

ACKNOWLEGMENTS

Should I or shouldn't I? That was the question I asked myself over and over when Moody Press suggested that I add *First and Goal* to my bookshelf of sports profiles books that already included *Safe at Home* and *Slam Dunk*. My difficulty did not arise from my reluctance to write about some of the best football players in the land. I relish that part of the process.

Nor did I doubt I would find dozens of NFL players who love the Lord Jesus Christ and are willing to talk about their devotion. The men on these pages display a robust faith, a love for people, and a zeal for the game of football.

I hesitated because I thought that for the next six months I would have to confront some tough, hard-nosed people labeled NFL public relations directors. I expected an ongoing battle to get their attention long enough to convince them to talk their players into granting interviews. Well, I finally decided to take on the project, and soon I received a pleasant surprise. The folks who work media relations in the NFL are very helpful.

So, for their efforts, I'd like to thank Scott Berchtold (Buffalo Bills), Lex Sant (Carolina Panthers), Dino Lucarelli (Cleveland Browns), James Petrylka (Detroit Lions), Rich Dalyrmple (Dallas Cowboys), Todd Starowitz and Nicole Kucharski (Indianapolis Colts), and Dave Auchter (Jacksonville Jaguars). Other PR managers who helped greatly were Stacey James (New England Patriots), Aaron Salkin (New York Giants), Derrick Boyco (Philadelphia Eagles), and Chip Namias (Tampa Bay Buccaneers). Also, my thanks to Mary Bednarz of the Junior Seau Foundation, who hooked me up with Junior; Kyle Rote for his help with Reggie White; and to Brent Jones and Ken Ruettgers for letting me get to them without any red tape.

Ken Ruettgers, a true gentleman and a fixture on the Green Bay offensive line, helped tremendously by writing a letter of recommendation I could share with all of the players.

Also, I need to acknowledge some sources of general, background information. Included in those resources were *Sports Spectrum* magazine and radio, *Sports Illustrated*, the media guides of the various NFL teams represented, and more helpful sites on the Internet than I could possibly name.

To three-time winning Super Bowl coach Joe Gibbs, thanks for carving out some time from your NASCAR schedule to kick the book off with your wisdom.

Finally, thanks to the Moody Press team. From James Bell, the editorial director, to Jim Vincent, the book editor, the Chicago crew has again been invaluable in guiding the development of this book—just as they were with *Safe at Home* and *Slam Dunk.*

INTRODUCTION

A Football Frenzy

America has gone bonkers for football.

Listen to any sports talk radio station. Read any sports magazine. Watch any sports report. Eventually they all come around to talking about football. And it doesn't have to be football season. Just as baseball talk once heated up long winters around the hot-stove league, now football talk steams up America's winter, spring, and even summer. During the late winter and early spring, it's the upcoming draft that stokes the fans' passions. In the off-season every team is a contender, and far too many teams are headed to the next Super Bowl.

During the summer, there may be a slight pause in the nation's ongoing football dialogue, but it picks up speed like a John Elway pass soon after July 4 as the players report to training camps to prepare for the next long campaign.

Admit it. You have a favorite football team. Probably two of them: one pro, one college. And that's not even mentioning the high school teams that dominate Friday night life in the USA every autumn.

And because you have at least one favorite team, you too spend some of your discretionary time staring at games on the tube and reading sports reports about your team. It's part of America's football frenzy. Perhaps you even surf the Internet looking for the latest stats on the team that gets your blood percolating—or talk about your squad's chances over a cup of java.

It can be a bit frightening—this all-out devotion to football. The game itself is dangerously close to becoming a religious experience in our land. Droves of people congregate on Sunday to pay homage, spending large amounts of money in voluntary support of the organization. Devoted fans center their lives around these energizing events each week, and sometimes they let the fortunes of the team dictate their mood for the next six days.

Yet among the men down on the field is a group who understand something that the die-hard fan might have somehow forgotten: The helmeted gladiators who toil between the lines deserve no more honor than the guy who paid $25 for a seat in Section C, Row 8, Seat 3. These men know that the only person who deserves our homage is Jesus Christ.

You can find men like that on almost any team in the NFL. They are men who may be bigger, stronger, faster than most of the male population in America. They may be able to throw, run, kick, tackle, block, and catch better than the guy up in the nosebleed section. And they may earn more money than 90 percent of the people who watch them play.

But they know they are no different, really. They know that they are sinners whose only hope for future security in heaven is wrapped up in trusting Jesus Christ for forgiveness. They know that He alone is worthy of adoration, and they give it to Him.

They realize that once they have accepted Christ, their source of true happiness is living according to God's Word. Their testimonies are robust and honest—stories of strong men who admit they have blown it and need forgiveness, but find comfort and a developing maturity through their Christian faith. And the testimonies come from some of the NFL's brightest stars: You will find seven Pro Bowl players among the ten veterans (more than four years in the league) in Part 1. Among the young warriors in Part 2, you'll meet the 1995 Rookie of the Year.

Some of these men you can't help but know about. Who hasn't heard the Reverend Reggie White talk about his faith? And who doesn't know how valuable Frank Reich's faith was to him when he orchestrated the NFL's greatest comeback ever? And how can you miss the God-directed humanitarianism of powerful linebacker Junior Seau?

Others of them you may know because they play for—or maybe against—your favorite team.

But once you've read about them, you'll not only be touched by their stories, but you'll also now have new stories to share when the subject at school or work turns to football. You'll be able to weave these players' faith stories into your own accounts of the highlights and headlines that dominate a country that has gone bonkers for football.

And the next time your favorite team has a first and goal inside the opposing team's 10-yard line, perhaps you'll think of these sixteen NFL players, whose first goal is to honor their Lord Jesus Christ.

It's time to kick off their testimonies.

PART ONE

THE VETERANS

Earnest Byner
Gaining a New Perspective

VITAL STATISTICS
Born September 15, 1962, in Milledgeville, Georgia
5 feet 10, 215 pounds
College: East Carolina
Position: Running Back
1996 team: Baltimore Ravens

CAREER HIGHLIGHTS

- Eleventh player in NFL history to record 1,000-yard seasons with two different teams (Cleveland and Washington)
- Selected to Pro Bowl twice (1990, 1991)
- Started at running back for the Redskins in the 1992 Super Bowl (XXVI)
- Had back-to-back 1,000-yard rushing seasons while with the Redskins (1990, 1991)
- 1983 AP college All-America honorable mention

WARMING UP

As the 1995 season neared the halfway point, Browns owner Art Modell dropped a bomb on the doghouse. He announced that he had accepted an offer from Baltimore to move the Browns from Ohio to Maryland.

To the people of northern Ohio, losing the Browns was unthinkable. These were fans who were clearly among the most devoted in the land. They had compiled the best TV ratings for their games of any NFL city in the country. They had filled ancient, windy, cold Municipal Stadium faithfully for years. They had created a fan persona by inventing the Dawg Pound. There could be absolutely nothing more the fans by the lake could do to show how much they loved the Browns.

But Art Modell felt he needed more money, Baltimore offered it, and the Browns, their fans, and fifty years of tradition were left out of the equation. In less than six months the Cleveland Browns would transform into the Baltimore Ravens.

As this controversy swirled around Lake Erie and Cuyahoga County, it swept away any chance the Browns had at putting together the season that was expected of them. Although they won three of their first four games, that was before Modell's missile hit its mark. After that, the team would win only two more games the rest of the way.

It was easy for the players to get caught up in the negative wrangling that took place throughout this nightmare season for Cleveland.

And the heat even got to Earnest Byner.

Earnest Byner

Many experts had forecast 1995 to be the year of the Cleveland Browns. Many picked the Browns to win their division, and others chose the team to go all the way to Super Bowl XXX. The Browns seemed poised to overtake their archrival, the Pittsburgh Steelers, in the quest for their first appearance in the Super Bowl.

One key to the resurgence of the Browns was Earnest Byner. Byner's postseason stats put him at or near the top in many categories among the Browns' running backs. His experience in the big games would come in handy should Cleveland, as expected, make it into the playoffs. The Browns knew they could count on Byner to provide leadership both on and off the field. He was coming off a 1994 season that saw him gain just 219 yards, far below the numbers he had put up during his early days as an NFL rusher, and the Browns were expecting 1995 to be a turnaround year for him as they raced to the playoffs.

Then the roof caved in.

The Browns players watched the football season disintegrate before their eyes. The devastation began with the midseason bomb dropped by Browns owner Art Modell. As the 1995 season neared the halfway point, Modell announced that he had accepted an offer from Baltimore to move the team from Ohio to Maryland.

More than a decade after Robert Irsay had moved the Baltimore Colts to Indianapolis under cover of night, Modell shocked the hometown fans with his plan to cart the Browns to Baltimore. To the people of northern Ohio, losing the Browns was unthinkable. These were fans who were clearly among the most devoted in the land. They had compiled the best TV ratings for their games of any NFL city in the country. They had filled ancient, windy, cold Municipal Stadium faithfully for years. They had created a fan persona by inventing the Dawg Pound. There could be absolutely nothing more the fans by the lake could do to show how much they loved the Browns.

But Art Modell felt he needed more money, Baltimore offered it, and the Browns, their fans, and fifty years of tradition were left out of the equation. In less than six months the Cleveland Browns would transform into the Baltimore Ravens.

As this controversy swirled around Lake Erie and Cuyahoga County, it swept away any chance the Browns had at putting together the season that was expected of them. Although they won three of their first four games, that was before Modell's missile hit its mark. After that, team members became so distracted by the controversy—and their own futures—that they would win only two more games the rest of the season.

It was easy for the players to get caught up in the negative wrangling that took place throughout this nightmare season for Cleveland. One well-known, high-paid player, for example, became disenchanted with the fans and began to say openly that the team's home was Baltimore.

And the heat even got to Earnest Byner.

Earnest Byner had known the hot breath of fan displeasure in Cleveland before. In perhaps the worst moment of his NFL career, Byner had the ball stripped from him just seconds before he crossed the goal line in a 1988 playoff game against the Denver Broncos. The Browns were driving to tie the score late in the game when the Broncos' Jeremiah Castille knocked the ball loose. Castille recovered the football, and the Broncos went on to win 38–33.

Castille's steal wiped out for Byner what should have been a career game, and it denied him the chance to cap it off with a heroic, game-tying TD. He had already scored two touchdowns and racked up 187 all-purpose yards, but any good memories of that game are always tempered by The Fumble.

Yet in 1995, here was a brand-new Earnest Byner. His inner life seemed at peace thanks to a spiritual decision he had made. Here was an Earnest Byner who had life and football under control. An Earnest Byner who would show class during the adverse circumstances of the Browns' planned desertion of Cleveland.

So much had happened to him between that 1988 AFC title game and the 1995 Season That Betrayed The Browns. The team had traded him in 1989 to the Washington Redskins. Earnest was in the middle of a string of 1,000-all-purpose-yards seasons with the Browns, and he was headed to a team with Super Bowl potential.

As a Redskin, Byner no longer had to answer questions about that fateful January against the Broncos. More important, as a Redskin he would soon make a decision that would affect him much more than any play on the football field ever could.

That decision had to do with something that had been on Byner's mind for a long time—ever since he was a kid growing up in Milledgeville, Georgia. Milledgeville seems like a pleasant enough town, as a summer destination of vacationers who enjoy its scenic, rolling hills and many recreational lakes. Located thirty miles northeast of Macon, Milledgeville was the capital of Georgia before the Civil War. Today it has a more casual existence as home of Georgia College and 17,000 residents. But for Earnest Byner, living arrangements in Milledgeville were "somewhat strange." Earnest and his oldest brother were raised by his grandmother, who lived right next door to his mother and Earnest's three other siblings.

"I grew up thinking that my grandmother was my mother," Byner recalls. "I can remember being told, and I can't remember by whom, that she was actually my grandmother."

In this confusing family setting young Earnest found stability and assurance in one area: going to church. "My grandmother was a Southern Baptist. She loved the Lord. She walked around the house singing Christian songs. We liked hearing her do that. We grew up going to church, so it was natural."

And because Grandmother Reeves was the most influential person in Earnest's life during those youthful years, her faith made an impact on his life. When he was twelve years old, Earnest joined his grandmother's church. "I was blessed to join the church at that age. I had a real nice grounding in the Bible."

But, as Earnest was to discover later, something was missing.

"Joining the church back home was not the same as giving your life over to Christ," he explains. "I can't remember actually hearing the plan of salvation at that time. When you join the church, you are looked at differently by the people, but you're not necessarily committed."

Now, after joining the Redskins and having the best year of his NFL career, it was time for that decision. It was 1990, and Byner would finish the season with 1,219 rushing yards, fourth in the league. He would be selected to the Pro Bowl team. Indeed, after taking over the full-time rushing chores on the tenth week of the season, he would average 100 yards and 26 carries a game during the final seven weeks of the campaign.

Yet not all was happy in Byner's life. Yes, his game was in such high gear that he would be named the NFC Offensive Player of the Month for December, even throwing his first career touchdown, hitting Ricky Sanders for 31 yards. But inwardly, he was struggling, and he didn't know why. It was decision time for the future Pro Bowler.

"I had been keeping a journal," Earnest begins. "In that journal, I had asked God, 'Have I sinned against anyone?' I asked Him that if I had sinned against anyone to forgive me."

Despite the success on the field, something was bugging the man from Georgia. "At the time, things seemed to be getting more and more hectic, especially with my job. Some difficult circumstances had come up dealing with people on the team. One bad thing happened and then another bad thing happened.

"I was just walking out in the yard one Monday night after we had played the Giants, and I looked up into the heavens. I can still see the stars now. I said, *What have I done for all this to happen?* The thought was driving me: *I must be doing something wrong for all these things to keep happening to me.*"

About two weeks later, an unusual scenario developed one day on the Redskins' practice field. The defense was going through their drills and Byner stood on the sideline as the offense waited their turn. Then one of the defenders, Tim Johnson, walked over to where Byner was. Hot, sweaty, and tired, Johnson leaned on his helmet and quoted to Byner 2 Corinthians 5:17, which says, "Therefore, if anyone is in Christ, he is a new creation; the old has gone, the new has come!"

Johnson's direct, simple approach to the gospel was an "eye-opener," Byner recalls. "I guess that was really the last straw as far as my making a commitment to the Lord. We talked a little bit then, but we couldn't talk long because I had to go do my drill. I said, 'We'll get together after practice.'

"We decided to get together that Saturday at the hotel where the team was staying on the night before the next game. That night Tim led me in a prayer of salvation. He talked to me about the seriousness of the decision I was about to make, that it wasn't just something to go into lightly, that it was a lifelong experience.

"I had gone to church all my life, but it wasn't about repenting and changing—and starting a life that was going to bear fruit."

Byner noticed a change in his life immediately, but he knew he had some growing to do. "It's a lifelong process, as TJ had told me."

He started making some changes that would speed the process.

First, he began to pick a new crowd to hang out with. Before he became a Christian, there were certain people that, as he says, "I feared, for no apparent reason other than that Satan was trying to keep me from them. I didn't fear them anymore—like the team chaplain and some of the other Christians on the team.

"As time progressed, God has given me more understanding," Earnest says. "I've become more of a leader as far as my belief goes: being able to witness, being able to encourage people, giving [of myself]. It's really been a tremendous change that has happened in my life. I owe it all to God. Without my salvation, my life wouldn't be anything."

Byner had an amazing, new perspective. Some would wonder how a star football player in the NFL could make such a statement. After all, a player's ego normally comes front and center with most players.

And it's not as though Earnest Byner had just appeared on the scene. He had been a football star and a leader for a long time, so for him to say that his life would be nothing without God represents a true commitment to his salvation.

Leadership and football had been the hallmarks of Byner's high school years. In fact, he was the senior class president at Baldwin High School in Milledgeville. "That was something else that was really natural for me. I had a girlfriend, who is now my wife, and she sort of talked me into running for class president. Up until then it wasn't something that I really thought about doing."

As the class president, he had to give a speech at graduation, a frightening experience for everyone who has ever had to address his peers, parents, and other principal people in life, right?

"No, actually I wasn't scared. My grandmother helped me with it. I was prepared. I had written the speech. I had gone over it.

"Also, one of my teachers helped me with it. She actually gave me one of her tricks. It was to have a stick in my hand, a small stick, and to just rub the stick while I was on the stage and while I was giving the speech. I did that, and it went well."

Another thing that went well for Byner in high school was his time on the football field. He doesn't like to take credit for his football exploits, only saying, "The Lord blessed me that anything I picked up, I've been able to do it well." So well that when Byner left, they retired his football jersey. He acknowledges that part of his strength comes from a certain God-given mental focus. "He's given me the mentality—the understanding about sports."

Earnest also credits his high school coach, who wouldn't let him throw away his ability in football to pursue something else.

"One time, I was getting ready to quit football, but the coach came and talked me out of quitting. My personality is that when I'm into something, I'm really into it.

"My coach, Andy Bentley, really took an interest in me. I played football, basketball, and ran track. I wanted to keep going with that, but spring football got in the way. I wanted to quit football so I could keep playing all the other sports. Coach Bentley talked me out of quitting."

Good thing. At Baldwin High, Byner played four positions (quarterback, tailback, safety, and linebacker). And he played them well. In his junior year he had his first 1,000-yard rushing season and was selected All-State.

Although Byner was not a Christian at the time, he feels strongly that his next decision—which college to attend—was led by God.

"My life has really been mapped out," he explains as he begins to tell what led him to East Carolina. "God really had His finger on each and every move.

"When I went to East Carolina, it was the only school that actually offered me a scholarship."

But he almost went to Georgia Tech. A neighboring school, Southwest High, had sent a tape of a game with Baldwin to Georgia Tech. A Tech coach noticed Byner and liked what he saw. That coach, Ed Emory, called Earnest and asked him to come visit the campus, which

Byner did. Tech, though, did not offer him a scholarship.

Soon afterward, Emory got the head coaching job at East Carolina. "One of the first things he did," Byner recalls, "was call me up. I took a visit up there and he offered me a scholarship. It was something that I believe was definitely directed by God. It was a blessing."

It was a divine blessing for Byner and an athletic blessing for the East Carolina Pirates. Coach Emory had a specific goal with his team, to "make EC into a powerhouse in Division I," Byner recalls.

By Byner's senior year, the Pirates were poised and ready to take on the challenge. "A lot of what he tried to do culminated for the guys who were his four-year starters," Byner says. Emory featured hard practices to help players shape up to play tough Division I-A schools. Summer practices began with four-a-day practices, then dropping to working out three times a day, and then two. "Coach worked us hard!" Byner remembers.

East Carolina had a fine season in Earnest's senior year. Byner was the team's leading rusher with 862 yards, and he was named an AP All-America honorable mention. The team compiled an 8–3 record, with all three of their losses coming at the hands of the Big Three Florida schools: Florida, Florida State, and eventual national champions, the Miami Hurricanes. His hard work and his impressive stats earned him a spot on Cleveland's draft chart. Although he did not go very high in the draft (tenth round, 280th overall selection), he had all he needed, and that was a chance in the NFL.

The stage was set for Earnest Byner, a young man who was not afraid of hard work and leadership roles, to make something worthwhile out of his opportunity. Here he was, a 5 feet 10 kid from Georgia, playing in the backfield where former greats Jim Brown and Leroy Kelly once scampered. It was his chance to make his own way—to give those dedicated Browns fans new thrills to cheer about.

In the final game of his rookie season, the fans got a taste of what was to come. The Browns were playing the Houston Oilers, and Earnest Byner ran wild. He rushed for 188 yards on 21 carries. It was the second most rushing yards ever recorded in one game by a Browns rookie, trailing only the great Jim Brown, who rambled for 237 yards in a game during his first year in 1957. Byner may have been number 280 on the draft roster, but he was vying for number 1 in the hearts of Cleveland fans.

As an established part of the Browns' machine, Byner became a full-time starter the next year, and he teamed up with rookie running mate Kevin Mack for a combined total of 2,104 yards. He and Mack were only the third backfield duo in NFL history to each gain at least 1,000 yards in the same season, and the paired the Browns into the 1985 playoffs. There Byner broke three Cleveland postseason records: most yards rushing, 161; longest run, 66 yards; and highest average per carry, an impressive 10 yards. Earnest Byner had come a long way from Baldwin High School. But he still had so far to go.

That year marked the high point statistically for Byner while with the Browns. An ankle injury and subsequent surgery limited his playing time in 1986, and even after that he never reestablished his running game in this first stint with Cleveland. The infamous fumble concluded the 1987 season, he had a better-than-average season in 1988, and then he arrived in Washington.

Tim Johnson's practice field witness and Earnest Byner's hotel room conversion came in the capital, as did his football career highlight. During the 1991 regular season, the Redskins had put together a remarkable 14–2 record. Byner had his second straight 1,000-yard season rushing with the 'Skins, was named to his second consecutive Pro Bowl, and selected to several All-Pro teams.

During the playoffs, Coach Joe Gibbs had his players ready and waiting. Quarterback Mark Rypien, Byner, and company pushed past the Atlanta Falcons 24–7. Then it was time to play the Detroit Lions. Winner goes to Minnesota for the Super Bowl. Loser goes home.

Surely for Byner, his thoughts went back a few years to the time the Browns came tantalizingly close to reaching the Big Show before falling.

Close would not describe this game. The Redskins annihilated the Lions 41–10, nearly repeating the 45–0 drubbing they had given Detroit in the first game of the season four months earlier. The 'Skins were in.

Two weeks later the Redskins won the Super Bowl, 37–24 over the Buffalo Bills. But the NFC championship victory over Detroit remained Byner's season—and career—highlight. "Winning the Super Bowl was a very outstanding moment, but I think winning the NFC championship was better. That was so exciting because I had been in that situation before, and we didn't make it."

Not that the Super Bowl was anticlimactic. Byner knew the importance of the event, and once the game began, the adrenaline kicked in. "I was really calm up until the first play. Then all of a sudden I realized it was millions of people watching."

Coach Gibbs's game plan may have helped him get over those jitters. On the first offensive play of the game, quarterback Mark Rypien handed off to Byner. "Being called upon to run the ball on the first play was my Super Bowl highlight. It was like an awakening."

Later, Byner scored the Redskins' first touchdown on a 10-yard pass from Rypien, and Washington's rout of the Bills was on.

It was Byner's last big hurrah with Washington. During the 1992 season, a bad back kept him from a third consecutive 1,000-yard record, and the 1993 season was a problem for everyone in Washington as the team began to rebuild. Byner's playing time was severely reduced, and he gained only 105 yards all year.

For this former All-Pro, it was especially difficult. "When I got benched in Washington, and there appeared to be no apparent reason for it, it was really tough for me. Sometimes I would drive to work and I didn't even want to get out of the car. One particular morning I sat there for a while, and finally I went on in.

"A lot of people came up and told me that they were being blessed by the way I was handling things. I wasn't pointing fingers in the paper and saying, 'I want to play' and all that stuff. But it was difficult for me."

Byner believes the situation gave him "a better dependence upon God." There's no question that the Earnest Byner of 1993 handled football's setbacks much better than the pre-Washington Earnest Byner could have. "After becoming a Christian, and becoming a follower of the teachings of Jesus, I handle difficulties by realizing that God is ultimately in control."

Byner recalled a recent Bible study he attended about the subject of the Holy Spirit and the fruit of the Spirit. From the study he concluded, "When God puts us in these different situations, He's trying to get us to see that we should demonstrate the fruit of the Spirit. The way that I've been helped by that is by becoming more and more dependent on God."

So it was a mature Byner, one with a new perspective, who confronted the fallout during the 1995 season, after Browns owner Art

Modell revealed his intentions to move the Browns out of Cleveland. The heat was on, and the players were feeling it.

According to a story in the *Willoughby (Ohio) News-Herald*, a group of reporters surrounded Byner in the locker room, asking him about the upcoming game with San Diego—and, of course, the Baltimore Debacle. One scribe asked Byner, "Is this the strangest month of your life? Could you ever imagine being in a situation like this?"

"There is no script for this, especially in the middle of the season," Earnest replied. "Day by day, moment by moment, that's the only thing we can do and trust this is all going to work out, regardless of the images we're faced with."

A second reporter then revised the first question, revealing one reason some athletes don't like to do interviews. He wanted to know if this was the "worst" month of Byner's life; he asked the running back to compare the moment with that forgettable episode long ago when Jeremiah Castille ruined the Browns' season and damaged Earnest's with the fumble recovery.

"Aw, c'mon," he replied. "You tell me, what was the worst month in your life?" Then he continued to bear down on the reporter, grilling him relentlessly.

Finally, the reporter meekly responded, "When my mother died."

"See, how was that for you?" Byner inquired, attempting to show the writer how these questions felt.

Byner walked away, and the writer turned to another player to ask more questions.

In the middle of that interview, Byner reappeared, offered his right hand in a handshake, and said, "Sorry about that. I shouldn't have said what I did." The scribe also apologized, and the two men shared a hug of forgiveness.

"Look at that," said Byner's teammate Tony Jones. "If we had more players like that, we'd be a better team."

Noting the scene, *News-Herald* writer Jeff Schudel commented, "Readers, please believe this observation after 18 years in professional locker rooms. For Byner to do what he did in front of teammates, who regard reporters as garbage can maggots, took more courage and conviction than playing with a broken bone."

For Earnest Byner, the difficulties surrounding the Cleveland Browns' lost season were trying and bothersome. But because of the boldness of his former teammate and current partner in ministry, Tim Johnson, and because of his growing faith in Jesus Christ, he has gained a new perspective that can help him turn even these situations into something good.

You don't have to be a long-suffering Browns' fan to know how important that is in life.

Q & A WITH EARNEST BYNER

Q: *As a pro football player, how do you keep from thinking more highly of yourself than you should?*

Earnest: I never have been the type of individual who really looked at the stats or got caught up in things that I accomplished—or was supposed to accomplish. I just look forward to going out and playing and enjoying the game. Most of all, I enjoyed winning, and it hurt tremendously to lose.

I think it was a God-given favor for me to not get caught up in the bragging.

The Bible speaks about bragging, and it says let other people talk good about you. You know, don't talk about yourself. When people do that, sometimes it's somewhat overwhelming. It even lets me know what I've done, because I sometimes don't know.

Q: *What service projects are you involved in?*

Earnest: Tim Johnson, Charles Mann, Art Monk, and I started the Good Samaritan Foundation. We try to help out people who don't have much by providing them with clothes and food.

I do limited speaking, but I'm about to start venturing out more. I feel it's time to really be more on the front lines in battle and to tell people about the goodness of God, the peace, the salvation, the love. That needs to be talked about. And [as football players], we're given an automatic platform. But you have to be spiritually ready too. You just can't jump out of the fire and start talking about Jesus.

God has been preparing me. My church, the Grace Covenant Church of Virginia, has helped. The minister has been able to come over to the house and teach me. Going to church and being fed the Word helps. Also, I have my own time with the Lord, doing different studies.

Q: *What special message do you like to share with people?*
Earnest: I tell them that they can be free from things that are bothering them on a consistent basis. God offers the freedom and the victory that's in Jesus, and He offers it to everybody. It's just a matter of accepting Jesus and living in a way that will glorify God. You're not just representing yourself, you're actually representing your Creator.

Q: *What is the toughest thing about being an NFL player?*
Earnest: There are a few of them, actually.

One is the physical part of the game—having to stay physically ready, in shape. After twelve years, to stay in shape is tough—to do the extra things that I didn't have to do when I was twenty-four.

The mental part for me now has been mostly given over to Christ. I can do the studying and all that stuff, but the relaxation and the mentality of why I play and how I play has all been changed.

Also, some of the mental games, mental hoops that we have to go through are tough. Like the coach feeling that he has to do things to get us to respond in the way that he wants. I don't like those games. I know they go on, but it's something we have to deal with.

Q: *What legacy do you want to leave in the NFL?*
Earnest: I want people to realize what makes the difference in this life that I've been given: Jesus Christ. And I want people to think: *He was a winner. He always gave his all. He always fought to the end.*

Howard Cross
Spread Too Thin?

VITAL STATISTICS

Born August 8, 1967, in Huntsville, Alabama
6 feet 5, 260 pounds
College: Alabama
Position: Tight End
1996 team: New York Giants

CAREER HIGHLIGHTS

- Has played in more than 100 consecutive games for the Giants
- Played in Super Bowl XXV win over Buffalo, catching four passes (1990)
- Caught first NFL TD pass against Seattle (1989)
- Won Jacobs trophy as top blocker in Southeastern Conference (1988)

WARMING UP

Big number 87 for the New York Giants is proof that a man with a soft heart for others can have a hard body that can become an intimidating force on the playing field. Cross tells a story on himself that reveals the ferocious competitive drive that burns inside him.

"A player spit on me during the game," Cross begins, careful not to reveal who the player was. "He was really aggravating me. He was really a mouthy player—some players are like that. I was kind of enjoying it, because if someone is like that, I want to play harder.

"Anyway, I was beating him, and he spit on me. So I lost it. It was like, 'I'm going to break his legs.' I'm screaming out loud at him. I'm standing between my huddle and his huddle, screaming at him.

"Then one of the players on his team came over to me and said, 'You're not representing Christ very well right now!' I stopped and looked at him.

"Then he said, 'Kick his tail! But don't be screaming and grandstanding. You don't have to scream and yell it. Just do it.'

"I stopped screaming and yelling, and I wore him out the rest of the day."

Howard Cross

To look at Howard Cross, you'd never think of him as being too worried about the word *thin*. After all, the man stands 6 feet 5 inches tall and weighs 260 pounds.

Big. Tough. Strong. Muscular. Massive. These are words you'd normally think of.

But *thin?* Not something Mr. Cross needs to worry about, you might think.

Yet spreading himself too thin is a serious concern of the New York Giants' veteran tight end. That's because Howard Cross has a big heart to go with that NFL body of his.

His big heart keeps tugging at him to help more people—to make an impact on more children. But his mind—and his Daytimer®—say he can't help everyone.

You see, Howard Cross is a man who knows that his privileged position as a football player in the NFL was given to him for a purpose—to make a difference in people who need help.

For this man with a Super Bowl ring, taking a message of hope to others helps remind him of the blessings he has. "Sometimes we need to remind people how blessed we are. If you ever want to remember that, just go to a children's hospital. Take a toy, take whatever you can, and see those kids. They've never done anything to hurt anybody. They've never had a chance to do something so wrong that they can be unforgiven. They're just kids. A lot of them are terminally ill, and they can't do anything.

"I went to see a little boy not long ago. He was so excited to see me, but he was dying. He said, 'Howard, it's good to see you, but I'm really tired. I need to rest.' I had to take a long drive after that."

But it's not only meeting with kids in hospitals that interests Cross as he seeks to help others. He also is involved in Athletes in Action, the American Diabetes Association, the Fellowship of Christian Athletes, and other ventures. Therein lie the possibilities of thinness.

In fact, a group that was trying to help Cross present himself to the public in the best possible way recommended that he attach himself to one singular cause as a marketing tool.

"I can't help everybody if I'm in one place," he protested.

"You're not going to be marketable," they countered.

"I don't know if I want to be marketable, then," Cross concluded.

Howard Cross is not looking to be some big McDonald's sign along the roadway of life; he'd prefer to be noticed as a role model who is involved in many areas, simply because there are many needs.

"A role model is someone who lives his life under a microscope," he says. "You know, every aspect of your life is exposed. A lot of people are watching you, and kids are modeling their lives after you. It's your *life*. You have to live it. And you're living it not just for yourself, but you're living for everybody around you.

"Kids especially need positive role models. When they don't have a chance to have role models at home, it's always great for some guy to come in and spend some time with them or be able to talk with them."

Some guy like the Giants' giant tight end.

One unfortunate result of our society's admiration of machismo is the false conclusion that a man who is kind, thoughtful, and caring is probably not especially tough. It's the thinking behind the old myth that Christians can't be tough competitors.

Big number 87 for the New York Giants is proof that a man with a soft heart for others can have a hard body that can become an intimidating force on the playing field. Cross tells a story on himself that reveals the ferocious, competitive drive that burns inside him.

"A player spit on me during the game," Cross begins, careful not to reveal who the player was. "He was really aggravating me. He was a mouthy player—some players are like that. I was kind of enjoying it, because if someone is like that, I want to play harder.

"Anyway, I was beating him, and he spit on me. So I lost it. It was like, 'I'm going to break his legs.' I'm screaming out loud at him. I'm standing between my huddle and his huddle, screaming at him.

"Then one of the players on his team came over to me and said, 'You're not representing Christ very well right now!' I stopped and looked at him.

"Then he said, 'Kick his tail! But don't be screaming and grandstanding. You don't have to scream and yell it. Just do it.' I stopped screaming and yelling, and I wore him out the rest of the day.

"The second time we played them, I was ready to jump all over this guy. We were out on the field, stretching. Apparently someone on the other team had spoken to him, because he came over before the game and apologized to me. He said, 'Man, that was wrong. I'm sorry, I shouldn't have done that.'"

Laughing now about the incident, Cross recalls telling the guy, "What! You just blew my game off! I don't have anything to play for!"

Howard Cross was only kidding. He has a lot to play for.

He's not only playing for the success of the Giants, but he's also playing for the honor of his family from New Hope, Alabama; for his wife, Joanna; for all those people he wants to help; and for his Lord and Savior Jesus Christ. That may sound like a long list of folks to represent—a list so long that it would spread the man too thin. But don't look for that to happen with a man as dedicated as Cross.

His dedication came early, as a result of living in a family that took its commitment to God seriously. For the Cross family, attending church was not an empty, once-a-week ritual. It was the center of their lives. With a grandfather who was a minister, a father who was a deacon, a mother and aunts in the choir, young Howard knew without a doubt where his roots lay.

"Living in the country in Alabama, maybe even the backwoods, church was the biggest event of the week for us," Cross says. "Everybody came together, not just from our town, but from other towns. We all got to hang out together. We heard a great sermon and had great singing. It was always exciting to go to church. All your social activities revolved around the church. If you had a barbecue, it was a church cookout."

So it was not at all unusual that at age thirteen, Howard found himself at the church with his cousin, Spencer, sitting smugly in the back of the sanctuary like any self-respecting teenager. "We thought we were grown-ups," Howard recalls. "I said to Spencer, 'I think I'm going to join the church this year. I'm just waiting for the right message.'"

When the message came, it was personal, relevant, and much more than joining a church. Sitting back there with Spencer, Howard heard the preacher talk about Jesus. He heard Reverend Moore say that Christ could be everything to everybody.

"Some of you have lost fathers and mothers; He can be to you your father or mother or brother," Reverend Moore said. "He will always be there when you need Him."

"I listened," Cross recalls. "It was really hitting home."

It hit especially hard because his parents had recently been separated, and Howard's mom was not living at home. When he heard that Jesus could help fill that void, he knew what he needed to do. That day, Howard accepted Jesus Christ as his Savior.

In addition to his relationship with Jesus, Cross also still finds strength in lessons passed down to him by his father. "My dad always pushed me toward success. He would say, 'You're going to make it. You're going to do good things. You're going to be great. But you've got to remember where you came from and what made you this way.'"

Today, Cross still credits his dad, Howard Sr., with being the most influential person in his life. "I spent most of my time with my dad," Howard Jr. says. "He was always there for me, taking care of me, pointing me in the right direction. He made sure that if I got too far out of line, he would put me back quick. He was just a good man."

One evidence of the power of this father-son relationship came during Howard's high school years. Howard Sr., who stood 6 feet 2 and tipped the scales at his son's current playing weight, didn't have to say much to get his boy's attention. "He was huge," Howard Jr. recalls. "All upper body."

So when he made a suggestion to his son, Howard took the initiative to follow through. He told Howard, "Son, I want you to get good grades."

"It wasn't just that I was going to finish school," the younger Cross recalls. "I was going to do great in school." And he did, finishing his academic career at New Hope High School with all A's. It wasn't until later that Howard discovered that his father had not finished high school.

Howard's good grades did not convince all of his teachers that he was major college material. In fact, some of his teachers thought he should attend a school with lower academic standards. The problem, Howard says, is that his school was small and part of a county system. "When you are in a county system in the South," he explains, "they are not academically compatible with the schools in the city."

Perhaps recalling his dad's push for excellence, Cross replied to those naysaying teachers, "I can go to any school in the nation if I want to."

And the one he wanted to go to was Alabama. "I saw Alabama play all the time on TV, and [during high school] I had played against their outstanding running back, Kerry Goode [now a strength and conditioning coach for the Giants]. I remember he scored six touchdowns against us in one game. Any way you can think of, he was scoring touchdowns. Intercepting and returning passes for touchdowns. He dropped back to punt once, and we fell back into coverage—and he ran for a touchdown. He was incredible.

"He went to Alabama to college, and I went there and talked with him. It seemed to be a real family atmosphere."

So, after a successful high school career both in the classroom and on the football field, Cross left New Hope for the University of Alabama.

As his teachers had warned, it was academically challenging. Typical of many good high school students, Cross learned that he had to study far differently now. "My biggest setback in high school was that I was smart. Being smart, I didn't really have to study. And not having to study paints an illustration that is not correct. Once you get to college, you have to study every day."

Cross succeeded in mastering the academic side of things, and he also got an added bonus while at Alabama. One of his professors gave him an insight that has helped him to this day to enjoy reading the Bible.

"Pat Herman was my English professor," Cross explains. "I took an upper-level English course, and he taught me not just to see words and phrases, but how to actually visualize—to see and experience what I was reading.

"He asked, 'What's your favorite book?'

"And I said, 'I'm always reading the Bible.'

"He would say, 'Put yourself there. Be there.' And I started reading that way. It opened it up for me.

"For instance, imagine being on a boat with Jesus. You're sitting there, and the water is rough and the wind is blowing and everything is going crazy. Imagine that Jesus gets up and quiets the wind, and then goes back to lie down. You're there thinking, *What kind of guy is this that even the wind and waves listen to Him?* You're there. You're on the boat. It's pretty moving."

Things also moved well for Cross on the football field during his years at Alabama. He started at tight end for three years for the Crimson Tide, and he played well enough to rack up such honors as All-Southeastern Conference and selection for the Senior Bowl All-Star Game.

For Cross, though, the highlight came early. In his freshman year, the Crimson Tide was not picked to have one of its best seasons. Preseason polls placed Alabama in the middle of the conference, and the Tide did not appear in any of the Top 20 polls, as they had just a few years earlier. Archrival Auburn, on the other hand, was supposed to put the heat on Florida for the SEC title.

That's why when Alabama squeaked out a tough victory over Auburn, Cross and his teammates knew that their year was a success. Alabama had better teams during Cross's time at Tuscaloosa, but they had no better game, in his opinion, than the one that closed out the 1985 regular season.

Alabama entered the contest a surprising 8–2–1 and Auburn was an equally strong 8–2. The Tigers were ahead of the Tide by a few spots in the polls. With just 37 seconds left in the game, Auburn was ahead 23–22.

Then Crimson Tide quarterback Mike Shula put on a clinic in ball movement. Starting on its own 12 yard line, Alabama moved the ball 53 yards in 31 seconds on three plays. With just six ticks left, Van Tiflin booted a 52-yard field goal to give Alabama a better record and Heart of Dixie bragging rights for another year.

Three years later, Cross was ready for the new challenge of the National Football League. Drafted by the Giants in the sixth round, Cross was able to move quickly into the lineup for New York. The reason for the quick adjustment, he contends, is the group of players he teamed up with in college.

"It was not really a big adjustment," he says. "I played with some great players at Alabama. I played with Derrick Thomas. I played with Cornelius Bennett and Jon Hand, who played several years in the NFL. Larry Roberts, who has two Super Bowl rings with the 49ers, was there. And Bobby Humphrey, who starred at running back for the Denver

Broncos. There was a ton of great players there with me at Alabama. I played against them a lot. The change wasn't that big coming to the pros. I just had to learn it. It was a job."

Shortly after he earned this job, he climbed rapidly to the pinnacle of football success. During his first year with the Giants, Cross played in all sixteen regular season games for Bill Parcells's 12–4 ball club. When Mark Bavaro went down with a knee injury, Cross was called on four times in a starting role. On a team that relied more on the running of O. J. Anderson than on the passing of Phil Simms, Cross averaged 17.8 yards per catch in his rookie season.

In his second year, the good times really began to roll. The Giants steamed through the playoffs behind substitute quarterback Jeff Hostetler and cruised right into Tampa for Super Bowl XXV. Along the way, Cross scored one touchdown in a playoff game against the Bears, and pulled down four receptions in the Super Bowl, including three catches in critical spots for first downs.

Super Bowl XXV, played in January 1991, was the Gulf War Super Bowl in Tampa. It became for America a time to take a break for something not as important as the fighting troops overseas— something that could draw the nation together. "It was so big at the time," Cross recalls. Super Bowl officials and the media had received threats that terrorists were going to blow up the stadium now that the United States was at war with Iraq. Now that the Persian Gulf War was underway, Americans felt uncertain but also patriotic.

"For a brief second, everyone kind of paused just to watch the game," Cross recalls. "I was awed by the whole thing. Whitney Houston singing the National Anthem, the whole nine yards."

With Houston singing, helicopters cruising securely overhead, and jets doing their flybys, the game had an even greater excitement and sense of expectancy than normal. The teams responded with one of the best Super Bowl contests ever. The Giants came out on top, 20–19, of course, when Buffalo's Scott Norwood missed a potential game-winning kick in the final seconds. Howard Cross and his teammates had won the Super Bowl, emblematic of the best professional football team in the land.

In the years since the Super Bowl, Cross has seen his playing time increase dramatically. In fact, he has not missed a game since the 1990 Super Bowl season. During the five years from 1991 through 1995, Cross averaged 23 receptions per year for the Giants.

This veteran NFL player doesn't stake his reputation on stats and salary increases as do so many of today's professional athletes. Sure, he enjoys possessing a Super Bowl ring, and he relishes the opportunities he has to help the Giants get back into the playoffs. But he also takes great interest in leaving a legacy that makes him stand out as much for being a good person as it does for being a good football player.

One of the ways he has left his mark on football is with what has become known as the Circle Prayer. After most games in the NFL now, fans watch as a group of players from both teams form a circle in the middle of the field, hold hands, and pray.

Howard Cross, among many others, was instrumental in the beginning stages of this phenomenon. As Cross tells it, the tradition began while he was a student at Alabama. "That started with a couple of guys. We had a nationally televised game against Penn State, and since we weren't going to be on TV too much, we thought it would be a good idea if we would just get together with a few players from the other team, kneel, and pray. Well, it got bigger and bigger at Alabama.

"When we came to the pros, I didn't say anything the first year. Then Dave Bratton, our chaplain, asked me if I wanted to do the same thing in the pros, and I said yes."

Now it is not uncommon to see ten or fifteen players gather after the game for Circle Prayer. Cross was one of its pioneers.

Another way Howard Cross is leaving a strong legacy in football is by being the right kind of person. A photographer who had been present during one of Cross's many benefit activities noticed the way he conducted himself and was impressed. Later, after she found out that Cross was a Christian, she had a chance to talk with him.

She told him, "I just want to say I could really see Christ in you. I talked to my husband [at the event] and said, 'I don't know, there's something about him.' Then I realized you're a Christian. You were just terrific with the kids, and you left a great impression with me. It's an inner love. You were just full of love and caring for the kids. It was Christ in you."

Mentioning kids to Howard Cross is like mentioning Republicans to Rush Limbaugh. Cross talks about children with love and understanding born out of his vast experience with them. "A lot of kids have great potential," Cross observes. "They're out there trying to figure out which way they want to go. I tell those kids, 'Look, you can't just be a good kid and go into a shell. You've got to be a good kid and stand out.'"

Because Cross plays in the Big Apple, he has ample opportunity to reach out to kids in New York City. And he knows that with all the crime and toughness they have to endure, there's a lot of talk among kids about who's the baddest kid and who's on the top of the heap. That's why Cross uses Mark 9:33–34 when he talks to city kids. In that passage, the disciples had been discussing who was the greatest among them. But then Jesus asked them what they were talking about. The disciples were embarrassed with what they had been discussing. Cross says he uses this verse to show kids that people are not perfect, and that they don't have to act so tough.

"Kids are having a hard time," he says. "They're getting a lot of the wrong images on TV. Unfortunately, they can't differentiate between fantasy and reality. I see so many talk shows that tell them it's OK to be that way. And nobody's really telling them that it's OK to be good kids."

Not true, Howard. You're telling them.

When Howard was thirteen years old, God came into his life in the person of Jesus Christ. Today, he has an interesting way of telling the audience—kids and adults alike—the difference between being a person who knows *about* God and one who really *knows* Him.

"A lot of people know who Lawrence Taylor is," Cross begins, mentioning his former teammate with the Giants. "They've seen LT on TV, sacking guys; they see him on TNN now. With the TV talk show, with his commentating on the games and such, people think they know him.

"The thing they know most about him is his football playing ability. And they know how many sacks he had, and how many times he's been to the Pro Bowl.

"You know, knowing about LT is great, but I actually know him. I know his kids. I know his wife. I know his big dog Max, unfortunately.

"I know Lawrence. Same thing with the Lord. It's not enough to know *about* Jesus; you have to *know* Jesus."

There cannot be a better message for anyone—football player or not—to convey to as many people as he can. And Howard Cross is determined to use every avenue possible to do so.

Let's just hope the big guy doesn't spread himself too thin in the process.

Q & A WITH HOWARD CROSS

Q: *Are we doing enough to help kids?*
Howard: We're inside the church, and all these great things are happening for us. We're receiving all these blessings. But outside that door, there's teen suicide and violence and stuff. And we're blind to that.

I'd like to think we have a connection. A lot of Christians would like to think that we are doing all we can. But there's a lot going on so close to us that it's right outside our door. But we haven't taken the time to get involved. As much as I do, there's still so much more.

Q: *What's your favorite Bible passage?*
Howard: Right now it's Romans 8:31: "What, then, shall we say in response to this? If God is for us, who can be against us?"

Q: *How did you meet your wife, Joanna?*
Howard: I met her when I was out on a date. She was working at a restaurant. I saw her, and I said, "Man, that's a really nice girl right there. Maybe one day I'll ask her out." When I got an opportunity, I did ask her out. Actually I had to ask her out several times before she said, "Yes." But she finally went out with me, and we fell in love.

Q: *How do you and Joanna stay strong spiritually?*
Howard: We go to church together, and we go to the husband/wife Bible study with our team. Joanna is a full-time student and she's doing some charity work, but we spend as much time as we can together in the Word and going to church. Those things help us stay spiritually connected.

Q: *How do you avoid the temptation that is so much a part of the life of an athlete?*
Howard: Sex and lust are a problem. Women may not even look at you until someone says, "He plays for the Giants." Then it changes. That really upsets me that we are targets like that.

But I can't see hurting Joanna. And I'm not going to do anything to hurt her.

If some temptation is really after me, Joanna says, "You need to pray. Or you need to pull out your CDs and listen to them." We have a lot of gospel music around, and that helps.

Q: *What advice do you have about dating?*
Howard: You have to be patient, because God has someone for you. It will help you not only emotionally and physically, but it will help you spiritually to have someone going in the same direction to lift you up when you're a little down; sometimes you need to guide someone. And if you wait and are patient, the Lord will send you someone.

When I was dating and looking around, you could always find someone who you liked, but it was hard to find everything you wanted. But I found out that I was looking in the wrong places—not just places like locations, but places in the person.

Sometimes you see a person and the first thing you notice is her face. You notice how she looks. And then you might notice her personality, but sometimes you have to ask about her spirituality. And I think that should be the first thing you look at when you're trying to find a mate.

Jim Harbaugh
Captain Courageous

VITAL STATISTICS

Born December 23, 1963, in Toledo, Ohio
6 feet 3, 215 pounds
College: University of Michigan
Position: Quarterback
1996 team: Indianapolis Colts

CAREER HIGHLIGHTS

- Earned highest passing rating in 1995 among all NFL quarterbacks, 106.9
- Named to the 1996 Pro Bowl team
- Selected in the first round of NFL draft (twenty-sixth player chosen)
- Set Michigan records for completions (387), completion percentage (62.4), and passing yardage (5,449)

WARMING UP

Finally, the Colts were in the playoffs again. Next stop? A date with the San Diego Chargers—at San Diego, where the Chargers had Junior Seau and rabid fans with the recent taste of the Super Bowl in their mouths. Indy had Captain Comeback and no Marshall Faulk, who ran one play, injured his knee, and took a seat.

Nobody expected the Colts to dominate as they did—winning 35–20 behind rookie Zack Crockett, who ran 147 yards to key the victory.

The unlikely quarterback had guided the unlikely team into contention for the AFC championship. As soon as the final gun sounded, reporters materialized in Harbaugh's presence to capture his response. What they got was a surprise.

Jim Harbaugh

He caught it!"
That was the immediate reaction of Indianapolis Colts fans everywhere at the end of an exciting AFC championship game when a long-distance Jim Harbaugh pass nestled in the arms of his Colts receiver. Instead, the Colts were losers, though they came within a chin strap of beating the Pittsburgh Steelers and going to the Super Bowl.

With just five ticks left on the scoreboard clock, Harbaugh attempted to do again what he had become known for around the National Football League—pulling victory out of the jaws of defeat. In this dream matchup with the Steelers—with a throwing hand that was marred by a dislocated finger—Harbaugh stepped back and fired an up-for-grabs pass into the end zone.

To get to the brink of victory in this game to decide who would play the Dallas Cowboys in the Super Bowl, Harbaugh had orchestrated another of his heroic comebacks. Earlier in the fourth quarter, the Steelers had led 13–9. Then Harbaugh hit Floyd Turner with a 47-yard touchdown pass to put the Colts in front 16–13. But the Steelers were not about to give up on their own dream. Rallying behind another quarterback who had proved that he could bring his team back, Neil O'Donnell, Pittsburgh scored with less than two minutes left in the game to take a 20–16 lead.

That set up the definitive moment.

The Colts drive began on their own 16 yard line. Later, Harbaugh would summarize the daunting task. "If we were going to get to the Super Bowl, we would have to go 84 yards in about a minute and a half without any time-outs. I thought we could do it."

The team did move downfield, but along the way Harbaugh took a couple of nasty hits. On one play, his throwing hand was smashed into his helmet, dislocating his ring finger. Another time, a different finger was gashed. "I was bleeding like a faucet," Harbaugh would describe it.

Under mounting pressure and with painful injuries, Harbaugh scrambled upfield with about 20 seconds left, gaining 11 yards and leaving the Colts 29 yards from the goal line. After tossing a pass into the ground to kill the clock, Harbaugh had only 5 seconds remaining.

The Cinderella team of the 1995 season had one final attempt to make that slipper fit and put the Colts into the Super Bowl for the first time since they had moved to Indianapolis. Not since 1971, as the Baltimore Colts, had the men with the horseshoe helmets attended the Super Bowl party.

In one last winner-take-all aerial, Harbaugh fired a high, sailing pass that seemed to hang in the late afternoon Pittsburgh air for minutes.

"When I let the ball go, I was concerned that I had thrown it too far," he says. He wanted to throw it five yards into the end zone and allow it to arc down toward one of his three receivers bunched together in the painted area.

Finally, the spiral floated toward the ground as a gaggle of Steelers and Colts reached skyward. The Steelers were flailing to bat the ball down; the Colts were reaching to grab it.

When the ensuing scramble settled, Aaron Bailey of the Colts lay on his back—with the ball in his hands.

For a single second that was as dramatic as any you'll see in sports, neither side knew who was going to the Super Bowl. Neither coach knew if he would be going home for the season or gearing up to play the NFC champions. Neither quarterback knew if he had led his team to another comeback win. Fans from both sides leaped skyward in celebration.

Then came the signal.

With a wave of his arms, the official told the tale. No good.

The Pittsburgh Steelers were in.

Jim Harbaugh and the Indianapolis Colts were out.

"I thought he caught it!" You could see the words on Jim Harbaugh's lips as he looked longingly into the end zone while expressing the wishful words that so many Colts fans would console each other with in the next few days.

For Jim Harbaugh, the greatest season of his nine-year pro football career had come to a heart-pounding, gut-wrenching end. Captain Comeback had come up one comeback short.

Accustomed as we are to the often bitter reaction professional athletes can have to situations that don't go their way, one could guess how Jim Harbaugh might respond to this sad, sad turn of events. He'd probably show remorse that would make a grown football fan cry. Or anger with the officials.

That, however, is not how Harbaugh responds to adversity. That's not how things affect him. He's far too thoughtful and intelligent for that.

Instead, Harbaugh looked beyond the disappointment of one pass that did not hit its mark and the lost opportunity to play in football's showcase event. He would face defeat as we wish all athletes would do. He would compliment his opponents, he would praise his God. And he would keep things in perspective about this fun game called football.

"It would seem to be one of the most difficult losses I've ever had, but it wasn't," Harbaugh recalls. "I walked off the field sad because we weren't going to the Super Bowl, but I was overjoyed that I had played in such a fun game. I felt blessed to have been in that position to play a game where I knew I had given it 100 percent.

"I was overjoyed afterward, and it is probably hard for people to imagine that. But I gave thanks to God just for being in that position."

That the Colts had found themselves in this position—just inches from the Super Bowl—surprised most football watchers. But as the team made its drive toward its date with destiny, Harbaugh's attitude toward his success became less and less surprising. He made it clear as Indianapolis marched toward this showdown at Three Rivers Stadium that there was more on his heart than winning games.

Not many football experts expected the Colts to be around for the January playoffs—and it certainly didn't appear that if they went that far they would move on the arm of Harbaugh. When the 1995 season began, the new quarterback in town, Craig Erickson, appeared to be Coach Ted Marchibroda's man behind center. The Colts had brought him in from Tampa Bay, where he had started fifteen games for the Buccaneers in 1994. Harbaugh, on the other hand, had played in just twelve Colt games, starting nine of them. Clearly, the job was Erickson's.

Harbaugh was not particularly happy with this turn of events. In fact, he contemplated retiring from football to follow in the footsteps of his dad, the head coach at Western Kentucky University, and become a coach. Instead, Jim chose to wait for his opportunity.

The wait wouldn't be long. When Erickson failed to produce in the team's first two games, Harbaugh came in to rescue the Colts. In the first game, against Cincinnati, he brought the team back only to see the Colts fall in overtime. On the following Sunday, Harbaugh dug the Colts out of another hole, and this time the horses won, defeating the Jets.

Jim Harbaugh's personal comeback had begun, and it would trigger some exciting Colt comebacks as the season galloped along. Now the starting quarterback, Harbaugh led the team past previously undefeated St. Louis and Miami. Twice during the first five games, he helped rescue Indy from 21-point deficits to win. Soon sportswriters would dub Harbaugh "Captain Comeback" for his tenacity and courage to hang in against the pass rush and point deficits.

Despite Harbaugh's success, ten games into the season the Colts stood at only 5 and 5—hardly indicative of a team headed for the conference championship. One of the problems that kept the Colts from putting higher numbers in the win column was an injury to Harbaugh. An aggravated groin pull reduced his playing time and his effectiveness as the Colts lost to Buffalo and New Orleans to fall from 5–3 to 5–5.

When Harbaugh returned to full strength, he put together some phenomenal numbers and gave the team an inside shot at a wild card slot for the playoffs. Thirteen games into the season, he was having the best year of his career, compiling a league-best 106.9 quarterback rating by completing 66.4 percent of his passes for 2,065 yards, 15 touchdowns, and only 4 interceptions. The Colts' record improved to 7–6.

But then another injury derailed the Harbaugh express. This time he suffered a knee injury in a game with Carolina and had to undergo surgery. For the first time in his career, he went under the knife. It was December 4, and with three games remaining on the schedule, Harbaugh felt a sense of urgency to get back to the team. He vowed to be on the field by December 17 against the San Diego Chargers.

He was, but it didn't make the difference and the Colts lost to the Thunderbolts, 27–24, to fall to 8–7. It would come down to a final game with the New England Patriots at home in the dome. In a low-scoring game, the Colts prevailed, 10–7. They had captured their first playoff berth since 1987.

Next stop, a date with the San Diego Chargers—at San Diego, where the Chargers had Junior Seau and rabid fans with the recent taste of the Super Bowl in their mouths. On their side of things, Indy had Captain Comeback and no Marshall Faulk, who ran one play, injured his knee, and took a seat.

Nobody expected the Colts to dominate as they did, winning 35–20 behind rookie Zack Crockett, who ran 147 yards to key the victory.

The unlikely quarterback had guided the unlikely team into contention for the AFC championship. As soon as the final gun sounded, reporters materialized in Harbaugh's presence to capture his response. What they got was a surprise. "I want to thank my Lord and Savior Jesus Christ," Harbaugh said boldly into the microphones.

To many people, this was a surprise revelation from Harbaugh. Unlike Reggie White or Jason Hanson or even the vanquished Junior Seau, Jim Harbaugh had not been noted for his outspoken witness for Jesus Christ. Perhaps it was the surprise element that brought so much attention to Harbaugh's proclamation.

He had suddenly awakened sports fans again to the value of Christian athletes reflecting the spotlight on Jesus.

"It wasn't anything that was planned," Harbaugh explains about his testimony after this game—and even his subsequent one after the Kansas City victory the next week. After that win, which was an even bigger surprise to Mel Kiper and other sports experts than the San Diego conquest, Harbaugh again let it be known that the source of his success was the Lord.

Continuing to explain his spontaneous witness, Harbaugh says, "They stuck a camera in front of me and a microphone, and asked me how I felt. It just kind of came out. I felt so much joy. I wanted to give thanks for it."

Jim Harbaugh has been a follower of Jesus Christ since August 1990. When he tells how the transformation took place, he reveals how powerful the work of the Holy Spirit is in a person's life, for Jim can't really name anyone who led him to faith.

"I was in training camp, and I just had an empty feeling," he explains. "I had it for a while, but I didn't really know why. On the surface, things seemed pretty good. I was playing football for the Bears and was doing what I wanted to do. I had even had some success. But nothing ever seemed to click. There always seemed to be something missing."

Although there was no single person or event that led Harbaugh to the Savior, a number of factors seemed to point the way for him.

First, there was his background, which included growing up going to Catholic schools, which exposed him to a knowledge of Jesus.

Second, there was the influence of Christian friends on the Bears. "I had started to go to some Bible studies with Mike Singletary, who was leading them at the time."

And third, and perhaps most important, were the prayers of Jim's brother, John, who is now a coach at the University of Cincinnati. "He is a Christian," Jim explains, "and he had been praying for me every day for the last five years."

Of course in that summer of 1990, when Harbaugh felt the gnawing need for God in his life, he didn't realize the effects of these forces. "Nobody really said anything to me. I didn't know where it came from. I just got down on my knees and asked Jesus to come into my life."

When Harbaugh spoke up for his Savior during the 1996 playoffs, he was revealing a heart that since 1990 had been growing steadily stronger in his faith. Strong enough to take the heat that might come from such a stance.

"I really had only a handful of negative letters," Harbaugh says about his remarks. "Most of the responses have been overwhelmingly positive. I've tried to read all of them and tried to respond to them, but it's been impossible. In most cases, people wanted to express their encouragement or their thanks."

Regular mail hasn't been the only way Harbaugh has been hearing from fans these days. He also has his own home page on America Online. During the 1995 season, he logged in with journal reports to fans several times, sharing his on-the-field experiences and giving fellow computer buffs such scoops as these: he enjoys playing chess with his teammates, and he spends some of his time reading Shakespeare with his teammates.

In the first five months or so that Harbaugh was on-line, he received more than 6,000 electronic messages from fans—many of them thanking him for testifying of his faith after the San Diego and Kansas City playoff victories.

Throughout the 1995 season, Harbaugh seemed to be having the time of his life. He was offensive player of the week a couple of times. He was named to the Pro Bowl and experienced a bit of *déjà vu* as his last-second heave into the end zone almost brought the 1996 AFC squad an upset victory. He was the most efficient passer in the league.

And he got married to Miah Burke, whom he had met five years earlier.

No wonder he said, in all the excitement following one of his play-off wins, "It's a wonderful life."

Life for Jim Harbaugh began in Toledo, Ohio, in 1963, but he didn't stay there long. In fact, as a kid growing up in the home of Jack Harbaugh, football coach, he didn't stay anywhere very long. From Perrysburg, which is a suburb of Toledo, the Harbaughs went to Eaton and later Xenia, as Papa Harbaugh coached Ohio high school football. Making the jump to college, Jack Harbaugh coached at Morehead State University in Kentucky, then at Bowling Green State University in Ohio. From BGSU, the family moved to Iowa, then Michigan, and finally to Palo Alto, California, and Stanford University.

"It didn't bother me to move around so much, but looking back on it, it would have been nice to have a hometown," Jim says about his growing-up days.

Despite the moving, there was one constant in the Harbaugh family: sports. By the time Jim reached high school, he had played hockey, baseball, basketball, and football. Interestingly, Jim grew to love hockey, watching "hockey night in Canada" on Michigan TV. "I learned to play hockey, and my sports hero at the time was Bobby Orr of the Boston Bruins. I liked his number."

Orr's number 4 jersey now hangs in the rafters at the Fleet Center in Boston, and Jim Harbaugh proudly sports that number for the Colts.

The other sport that attracted Jim Harbaugh in his youth was basketball. "I was better at basketball," he claims.

Harbaugh's high school career was split between two schools. For the first two years, he attended Ann Arbor Pioneer High School, just across the street from his dad's office at the time—Michigan Stadium. His dad was an assistant coach under Bo Schembechler at the time.

But then Stanford called, and the Harbaughs were off to Palo Alto, where Jim finished his high school days as an average student. As Jim began to consider his college education, the choice seemed to be tough. After all, his dad had coached at five major colleges, and Jim had been all-league in baseball, basketball, and football. For Harbaugh, though, there was a factor that not many people have in their favor.

He may have been a better basketball player in high school ("I received more honors in basketball than I did in football"), but when it came down to decision time, no factor could be much more influential than this: "Bo said he wanted me."

Anyone familiar with the tradition of Michigan football in the '70s and '80s knows that there can be no sweeter words in football parlance than "Bo said he wanted me." Notre Dame is nice with its golden dome and strong tradition. You can't beat the weather at USC. And no state stands behind its team like Nebraska. But if Bo Schembechler says he wants you, maize and blue suddenly become your favorite colors. The University of Michigan and its fabled head coach called, and Harbaugh turned down feelers from Arizona, Wisconsin, and, yes, even Dad's home base, Stanford.

Little did Jim know what it would all lead to when he unpacked his bags in Ann Arbor. His expectations were small, and the future was unknown. "I was just looking for a scholarship. I wanted to get my schooling paid for. I didn't really think at that time that I'd be good enough to make a career out of it."

While at Michigan, Harbaugh went far beyond his expectations as he guided the Wolverines for four years. After redshirting his freshman year, he led the team to a Sugar Bowl berth in his first year as quarterback.

His sophomore season began well as he and the Maize and Blue compiled a 3–1 record. Then he broke his arm.

What was a setback for his football career became an asset in the classroom. A communications major, Harbaugh hadn't paid much attention to academic endeavors in his first two years. But the broken arm woke him up to the possibilities that he was missing.

"When I broke my arm and wasn't playing football for a half a year, I got into my schoolwork. I started to study pretty well. I had a semester when I got a 4.0 GPA, and I thought that was really cool. When I started to do well in the classroom, I began to put more effort into it." His Academic All-Big Ten honor as a senior demonstrated how seriously he had begun to take academics.

Back on the field for his third year of eligibility, Harbaugh began to show America what would become his trademark throughout his career: passing efficiency. He led the NCAA in that department while directing the Wolverines to a 10–1–1 mark and a date in the Fiesta Bowl. By leading Michigan past Nebraska 27–23, Harbaugh secured for Michigan the number two spot in the final polls behind Barry Switzer's Oklahoma Sooners.

The highlight of that year for Harbaugh, though, was the Wolverines' victory over rival Ohio State. "I threw a 77-yard pass toward the end of the contest that won the game. That is my biggest thrill on the field for Michigan," Harbaugh says.

But he wasn't done. Harbaugh's senior year was another highlight-film campaign. Included in the mix that season was a thrilling 24–23 win over Notre Dame. Harbaugh was 15 for 23 passing for 239 yards and a touchdown.

After that performance, the man who wanted Harbaugh five years earlier said, "There is no quarterback in America I'd rather go into the season with and have run my team than Jim Harbaugh." Bo certainly knows.

Although the season ended with a 22–15 loss to Arizona State in the Rose Bowl, the season was extremely successful for Harbaugh. He ended his career with the second most completions in Michigan history, was named All-Big Ten, set a school record for completions, attempts, and yardage in one season, and best of all, set himself up for possible inclusion in the draft in April.

And Bo Schembechler, who embraced the adage "When a quarterback goes back to pass, three things can happen and two of them are bad," knew Harbaugh was different. Bo showed that with the right kind of quarterback you can gain yardage without the fear of interceptions. It was a great combination of cautious coach and careful quarterback.

"I just loved Michigan," Harbaugh says of his days in Ann Arbor. "When I talk to people who went there, I've yet to run across anybody who didn't like it. It was a great place to go to college, but to play in front of 100,000 people was incredible. I played for a great coach— someone I truly loved."

The question is, can Jim Harbaugh say the same thing about the next person he played for? In the 1987 draft, Harbaugh was chosen by the Chicago Bears in the first round, 26th pick. He linked up with fiery coach Mike Ditka and began as backup to Jim McMahon. Harbaugh rode the bench most of the first two years, before getting more playing time with each season. "I believed in myself," he says of his extended bench time. "I really had a lot of fun in those first couple of years. I wasn't playing, but I had some great friends on the team."

By 1990, he was the Bears's top starter, getting the call fourteen times. In 1992 and 1993, he started 31 of the Bears's 32 games, while compiling some impressive statistics. Yet the Bears weren't winning, and as always happens, the quarterback carries a heavy share of the blame. "I got booed constantly," Harbaugh says. "There was a lot of negative press."

And then there was that incident on the sidelines with Mike Ditka in 1992. The volatile coach was incensed at his quarterback for an interception he threw, and he proceeded to lay into Harbaugh in front of the team, the TV cameras, and the whole country. "That was a rough period," Harbaugh admits, "but I just kept going, trying to do my best."

Overall, though, the experience was positive for Harbaugh. "I enjoyed Chicago. The tradition is strong, and playing in Soldier Field is special."

But it was still time to go in 1994 when the Colts signed Harbaugh as a free agent. "When I left Chicago, I was on pretty bad terms," Harbaugh admits.

Even coming to a new team, though, didn't bring an end to the residual feelings that had accumulated in the Windy City. "It took me probably a year to pull out of that whole Chicago thing," Harbaugh says.

In other words, for Harbaugh to become Captain Comeback for the Colts, he had to make a personal comeback from the difficulties that struck him down in Chicago. In his favor, as he began his career in Indianapolis, was the confidence of his coach. Ted Marchibroda said before the 1994 season, "Jim has established himself as our leader. He makes good decisions on the field. I'm very confident he can help us have a successful season."

Things looked promising as the 1994 season began. During the preseason, Harbaugh led the Colts to a 4–0 record. And when they took the first game against Houston 45–21, the Colts seemed to be for real.

Not yet. Three straight losses brought the team back to reality, yet the team never lost even two in a row again the rest of the way. An 8–8 season kept the Colts out of the playoffs, but the team knew how far they had come from 1993 when they had finished 4–12, uncomfortably on the bottom of the pile in the AFC Eastern Division.

The stage was set for 1995 and the emergence of Jim Harbaugh as one of the league's premier quarterbacks. He would have to climb back into the starting quarterback role. He would have to extricate the Colts from the wrong end of some scores. And he would have to continue bringing Indianapolis back from its ten-year playoff drought. Anybody who can do all that should qualify to be called Captain Comeback.

But perhaps the greatest thing Harbaugh did in this season of success was to bring attention to Someone who is going to return in the greatest comeback of all time—Jesus Christ.

When He comes back, there will be no doubt who the winner is.

Q & A WITH JIM HARBAUGH

Q: *What was your biggest thrill while at the University of Michigan?*
Jim: Being elected captain of the football team in my senior year.

Q: *What difference has it made in your life to know the Lord Jesus as Savior?*
Jim: It's changed my priorities. I grew up thinking that football was the most important thing and that people would like me because of how well I did as a football player. Now I realize that there's Someone who loves me more than it's possible to describe. It's a love that is unconditional.

Q: *What do you do to keep strong spiritually?*
Jim: When I first became a Christian, I read the Bible from cover to cover. That really gave me an understanding of the Bible. I think everybody needs to read the Bible on his own. It has also helped to have a church that has given me guidance. Plus our team Bible studies and our chapels. That type of fellowship is helpful.

Q: *What Scripture passage have you found to be most helpful to you?*
Jim: Philippians 4:6: "Do not be anxious about anything, but in everything, by prayer and petition, with thanksgiving, present your requests to God."

Q: *What kinds of people-helping ministries are you involved in?*
Jim: I like to get involved with Fellowship of Christian Athletes. I think it's a great outreach to high school and college athletes. Also, I like to work with Campus Crusade for Christ. I work with Helping Hands Ministry. Our team chaplain Ken Johnson does this. It's an inner-city ministry. He talks to elementary schools, puts on skits, and helps families here in Indianapolis. And I have my own foundation in Michigan that helps in some schools in the Ann Arbor area.

Q: *What kind of legacy do you want to leave in the NFL?*
Jim: I want to be a good role model for Jesus Christ.

Brent Jones
The Comeback Kid

VITAL STATISTICS

Born February 12, 1963, in San Jose, California
6 feet 4, 230 pounds
College: University of Santa Clara
Position: Tight End
1996 team: San Francisco 49ers

CAREER HIGHLIGHTS

- Selected to three Pro Bowls (1992–1994)
- Led NFC tight ends with 68 receptions (1993)
- Played in Super Bowl XXIV, catching one TD pass (1990)
- Named college All-American (1985; Division II)

WARMING UP

At age twenty-three, Brent Jones was a washed-up pro. His neck was still not well, and he knew why the team was worried. "When you have a neck injury in football, it's not something a whole lot of people are going to take a chance on. The last thing you want is a kid to come into your camp, get hurt, and have to be paid all year. Still, I was pretty devastated."

He was ready and willing to put his economics degree to work and leave football. "I knew my education was something I could fall back on. Clearly, you have to put yourself in the position to succeed. Having that degree put me in that position."

That's when the team he wanted to play for called. The San Francisco 49ers were on the line.

Brent Jones

I t was one of those teeth-jarring, head-snapping, chest-smashing tackles that safeties seem to relish and tight ends wake up in a cold sweat
fearing. And Brent Jones was on the receiving end of it. On October
1, 1995, in front of a cheering home crowd, the 49er receiver ran across
the middle of the field, looking for a tight spiral from quarterback Steve
Young. His eyes riveted on the ball and his arms reaching out for it,
Jones was in that vulnerable zone for a good old-fashioned collision.

As defensive backs are inclined to do, New York Giants' safety Ven-
cie Glenn timed his hit to crush Jones just after the ball touched his
hands. Then, with a force that would send most civilian-clothes-wearing
people to the hospital or worse, Glenn blasted into Jones.

The pass was complete for a 49er 10-yard gainer, but Jones would
go no farther. He was stopped in his tracks by the thunderous hit. No
flags were thrown. It was just another smash-mouth football play.

Or was it?

After the game, 49er players spoke up. Steve Young, who threw
the ball and had a great view of the impact, said, "Brent took what I
thought was a life-threatening shot."

He even equated it to a 1978 hit that left a New England Patriot
receiver paralyzed. "That's a Darryl Stingley hit," Young told reporters.
"And it's wrong." Later, he watched the hit on film and called it "chill-
ing."

Whether Brent Jones's monster tackle at the hands of Glenn was a

fair hit is open for debate, but what is unarguable is that Jones has survived an incredible slate of hits and hurts to hang around this long in the
NFL. If Colt quarterback Jim Harbaugh is Captain Comeback, then 49er
tight end Brent Jones qualifies as the Comeback Kid. He has come back
from adversity from way back—first as a high school sophomore playing
second-string receiver, and later as a recent college graduate crunched
in a different violent collision.

That collision came as Brent was driving along a street in San Jose,
California, on Mother's Day 1986. This time it was not Brent Jones who
was coming over the middle; it was a drunk driver who was operating
his car on a suspended license who crossed the middle.

As Jones was negotiating a narrow street near his house, the sus-
pended-license guy weaved across the center line and hit Jones's car
head-on. The collision sent Brent and his girlfriend, Dana, to the hospital. Investigating police officers later told Jones that if he and his girlfriend had not been wearing seat belts, they would have been killed.

As it was, Dana took the brunt of the hit, which dislocated a shoulder and broke her jaw. It would take several operations to put her jaw
back in working order. And for Brent, the accident left him with a herniated disc in his neck.

Car accident injuries can restrict any person's job performance, but
for football star Jones the concern went beyond the norm. Just a week
earlier, he had signed a contract to play tight end for the Pittsburgh
Steelers. And a herniated disc is not what a rookie wants to take to training camp with him when he's trying to make the team.

Especially a rookie with Brent Jones's up-and-down football background. For Jones had been a non-starter on the high school varsity,
with no hopes of playing pro football. Throughout his prep career at
Leland High School in San Jose, Brent Jones was "nothing more than a
second-string wide receiver," as he describes himself. With nagging
injuries in his sophomore and junior seasons, he didn't have the experience the other receivers had. "My coaches kind of liked the guys who
had paid their dues. I wasn't one of them," he explained.

Fortunately for his sports career, though, Jones was good enough
in baseball to attract the attention of some college coaches. When the
University of Santa Clara, a Division II school, offered him a scholarship,
he jumped at the opportunity. In fact, they offered him both a partial
baseball scholarship and a partial football scholarship.

How could a second-string wide receiver in high school get a football scholarship in college? According to Jones, it was only because "God was working in my life. There is really no other way. An assistant at Santa Clara, Terry Malley, whose dad was the head coach, was substitute teaching at our high school. We played some basketball and volleyball together, and he thought I showed potential as a football player. He told his dad about me, and I got a partial scholarship."

So, when Jones went off to college at Santa Clara, he went with the feeling that God definitely had His hand of direction on him. For Jones, this open relationship with God had begun a couple of years earlier during his sophomore year of high school.

"I started going to a club called Young Life," he explains. "My friends were going, and the captains of the football team were leading it, so I thought I'd go. Our leaders challenged us throughout the year about having a relationship with Christ. At first, I said, 'Yeah, whatever.' But toward the end of the year I really started to listen. I realized that there was a void in my life. In May of my sophomore year I prayed to accept Jesus Christ into my life."

While at Santa Clara, Jones continued to grow both spiritually and athletically. Although he had not originally planned to play college football, someone saw some potential in him, and he gave it his best shot. It was the beginning of a football career that would take him far beyond what anyone could ever hope. And it would turn out to be the downfall of his baseball career and any dreams of being a big leaguer.

Despite a good freshman year on the diamond, a gridiron injury the following fall spelled the end of his career with the bat. "When I dislocated my shoulder during the football season, the baseball coach took away my baseball scholarship," Jones recounts. "And that pretty much ended my baseball career."

The injury, though, was not career-threatening in relation to football. Jones had redshirted his first year, so this injury came during his second year at Santa Clara and his initial one on the team. By now, people had begun to notice his ability to catch the ball. After his second year with Santa Clara, the coaching staff switched him from wide receiver to tight end. "That transition was a highlight," Jones says. "It made me think about the possibility of playing professional football. As far off as that idea seemed, it was really an inspiration to me."

Once he switched to tight end, the doors began to open. First, in year three at Santa Clara, Jones was named to the All-Western Football Conference team. In his senior year, he was named an All-American and selected to play in the East-West Shrine Game.

By now it was time for this former high school bench warmer to get his big chance. It was not the Major League Baseball draft he once dreamed of. It was the National Football League draft, and Jones was pretty confident he had earned his shot at the big show.

"I was sure I was going to be drafted, but looking back on it, I don't know if I should have been. There were teams saying they'd take me maybe in the second or third round. But I discovered that they weren't looking for tight ends. I think I was the second tight end that went." When the second player at a position is drafted with the 135th pick, it's a clear signal that the line of people wanting to pick a player like that is very short.

He wanted to be chosen by San Francisco. "I didn't want to leave the Bay Area," he recalls. What he got was Pittsburgh.

And what Pittsburgh got was a hard-working, straight-laced young man they couldn't use. Or at least not in their timetable.

When training camp rolled around for the 1986 season, the Steelers' young tight end was not ready to play. The May auto accident was taking a continuing toll on Jones, and his neck had not recovered. The Steelers put him on the injured reserved list and started the season assuring Jones, "We're going to be patient with you. Whatever it takes." A month later, though, they changed their tune. Now they were telling Jones that they were releasing him.

At age twenty-three, Jones was a washed-up pro. His neck was still not well, and he knew why the team was worried. "When you have a neck injury in football, it's not something a whole lot of people are going to take a chance on. The last thing you want is a kid to come into your camp, get hurt, and have to be paid all year. Still, I was pretty devastated."

One consolation Jones had at the time was that he had completed his academic studies. "I had a degree from Santa Clara in economics, but I had no direction. I was just trusting God that something would happen.

"I knew my education was something I could fall back on. Clearly, you have to put yourself in the position to succeed. Having that degree put me in that position."

That's when the team he wanted to play for called. The San Francisco 49ers signed Jones for a contract that would start in 1987. It was still the middle of the 1986 season, and he would have to wait until training camp the following summer to see if he could play for San Francisco.

In training camp, though, his chance of making the team seemed as great as that of someone surviving a leap from the Golden Gate Bridge. "That was back when you went to camp with 130 to 140 guys. I went in as the eighth-string tight end." He had gone from second-string in high school to All-American in college and now eighth-string with the 49ers.

Of course, performance counts, and Jones had a great training camp. "I had to do everything right just to get the opportunity of getting looked at, and then it was just barely enough," Jones recalls. "I actually felt like I couldn't drop any passes."

But make the San Francisco 49ers he did—as a third tight end. The Comeback Kid had caught the coaches' attention and now hung on for his big break. "They still had Russ Francis and a couple of other guys, but they kept me on injured reserve. They wanted to hide me and let me get familiar with the system. In the middle of the season, they let Francis go, and they took me off IR."

Finally, on December 4, 1987, at age twenty-four, Brent Jones was a *bona fide* pro football player. His first regular season with the Niners lasted four games, in which he caught two passes for 35 yards. He was beginning to earn his keep as a pro football player.

On January 9, 1988, the Niners went up against the Minnesota Vikings in a game at Candlestick Park. Jones went into the game at tight end and caught a pass for 7 yards. It was the last 7 yards he would get for a long time. Once again a hard hit took its toll on Jones. The defensive back hit Jones and snapped his knee, blowing out his anterior cruciate ligament (ACL).

In the late '80s, ACL injuries often meant the end of the road for pro athletes. For Jones, the old story seemed to be playing a rerun in his life. "The team said it was pretty much over for me," Jones recalls. "But I never thought about giving up. The thought I had was that it would be given up for me. I was going to go as far as I could with it.

"I had my wife there to support me [Dana and he had married during the months prior to the 1987 season], and we just knew that God had a plan one way or the other. He brought us through everything else.

"When I started practicing again, my knee would swell up pretty bad, and not do very well. But I was making it through practice." During their first exhibition game, played in London, Jones fielded a kickoff and was hit pretty hard. Jones had injured his other knee. No surgery was needed, but a recovering Jones played little. Soon it was time for the final cuts.

"I went in and talked to Bill Walsh, and he said I should get on with my life because they were only going to keep two tight ends, and I wasn't one of them. So that was it for me. It was crushing."

Once more, Jones began thinking about how to use that degree in economics from Santa Clara. He had had his day in the sun—playing in five NFL games. Not many people can say that. Perhaps it was time to forget about football. Jones began to prepare for his real estate licensing test.

Yet the Comeback Kid wasn't done yet. The Niner team doctor had tended Jones when the physician was team doctor at the University of Santa Clara. He now convinced the 49er brass to keep Jones on the injured reserve list instead of cutting him loose. A few weeks later, John Frank, the team's starting tight end, broke his hand. That led to the Niners calling Jones up to the team again. It wasn't a Hall of Fame year for Jones in 1988—11 games, 8 catches, 57 yards, 2 touchdowns—but it was better than peddling houses.

And it was just the springboard he needed, for by the time the 1989 season rolled around, Brent Jones had the coaching staff's attention. In 1989, Jones started at tight end for the 49ers in all sixteen regular season games.

In the 1989 postseason, Jones flourished; in each of the three 49ers playoff games, he scored a touchdown. In the NFC Divisional Playoff game against Minnesota he scored on an 8-yard pass; in the NFC championship game he caught a 20-yard TD pass against the Rams. And then came the big one. On January 28, he caught his first Super Bowl catch—a 7-yard TD reception.

Brent Jones, who just a year and a half earlier had been told that his career as a football player was over, had completed a remarkable season. In all, the Comeback Kid had caught 48 passes for more than 500 yards and 7 touchdowns, and he had scored a TD in the Super Bowl, a play that he calls "the single most important moment" of his career.

It was just the beginning for Jones.

In 1990, he set a new team record for receiving yards by a tight end with 747 yards. And in one game, against Atlanta, he rambled for 125 yards on 5 catches—his best individual performance as a pro. He was having the kind of year that gets guys into the Pro Bowl. And it nearly got him into the showcase of NFL talent.

And it would have, had it not been for the NFL itself.

"We lost the NFC championship game that year to the Giants," says Jones as he tells of nearly making it to his first Pro Bowl. "Our coaches were the coaches in the Pro Bowl, and I thought I was going to go. I led all the NFL tight ends in catches and touchdowns. But I didn't get it, and I was just so down.

"A week before the Pro Bowl, our public relations guy called and said, 'Hey, nobody is supposed to know this, but start packing your bags.' Our coaches had one pick, and they were picking me. But then the league called them, and said, 'No, you have to pick a linebacker.' Nowadays, you can pick whoever you want, but that was back when you had to pick a linebacker. Coach George Seifert went crazy and yelled at the league and said, 'We're not picking anybody. You pick them.' So they picked somebody else."

By 1992, though, the Pro Bowl question was no longer debatable. After catching 45 passes for 628 yards and 4 touchdowns that year, Jones was named to his first postseason all-star game. The next two seasons also saw him earn a trip to Hawaii, and in 1994, he was named a starter on the team for the first time.

The Comeback Kid had come a long way from that first tryout with the Niners, when he was behind seven other tight ends just to make the team.

But there are other areas of progress in Jones's life that he is just as happy about as his progress as a football player. For instance, he and his good friend Steve Wallace, who became a member of the 49ers in 1986, were largely responsible for starting the team Bible study. "We were the only two guys in the Bible study for a year," Jones recalls.

Their relationship itself was another highlight for Jones, who expressed deep regret in early 1996 when he heard that Wallace had been released from the team.

"Over the years, we spent a lot of time together," Jones says of

Wallace and himself. "We used to go out to lunch or go to each other's room for Bible study and prayer. Also we were part of an accountability group that met the night before our games."

Another, more out-front activity Jones and other Christians are involved in is Circle Prayer. Often a dozen or more players from both teams meet on the football field to pray after game's end. This idea, which has caught on around the league, was first instituted with players from the 49ers and the New York Giants. (See Howard Cross's story.) For Jones, it has been a thrill to see this new way of acknowledging God's place in his heart and in the hearts of others in the league.

The life of an NFL player is often a roller coaster, marked by the valleys of injury and lack of playing time and the hilltops of success like winning the Super Bowl. Those who have put their faith in the Savior and who acknowledge God's role in their lives have an added resource in the midst of pro football's trials. Jones has ridden that coaster ride, and he knows how vital his relationship with God is in negotiating the ups and downs.

"It's my faith that has helped me keep my sanity. Otherwise I couldn't do it. I probably would have gone out of my mind a long time ago. But just knowing God has a plan for you gives you that peace. I can just work as hard as I can with rehab after an injury. If this isn't where God wants me, then I'll be somewhere else.

"I was clearly not a model football player to begin with, so I figured I'd been blessed with all that, so He can lead me wherever He wants.

"Hey, God is in control, and if it was all over right now, I know I've had a lot of great years, I've done something not a lot of people have done, and I've fulfilled a lifelong dream.

"That doesn't mean you don't question the tough times, the frustration, the painful rehab and surgeries—all the stuff it would be nicer to do without.

"We stuck together as a family. My wife was always there, encouraging me and saying, 'Hey, we've been here before.' We were in that car accident, so we can go through anything."

Brent Jones has taken his share of hits as his football career has taken its meandering course toward greatness. From that car accident in 1986 to the ACL injuries to a broken ankle to a variety of other bumps and bruises, he has continued to get back up to his feet by keeping his knees on the ground. Through prayer, a faithful wife, and an omnipotent God, Jones has transformed himself into one of the best tight ends in the game. Not so he can bask in Super Bowl glory or revel in Pro Bowl fame, but so he could return the glory to God.

The Comeback Kid knows one day he will hang up the knee braces and hip pads, but until then, he will keep taking those hits. If anybody can take a hit and keep coming back, giving you his best, it's Brent Jones. It's not hard to see what a great catch San Francisco made when they took a chance on this long shot of a tight end back in 1986. If anybody can take a hit and keeping giving you his best, it's Brent Jones.

Q & A WITH BRENT JONES

Q: *How would you like to be remembered as an NFL player?*
Brent: I would like to be remembered as a guy who worked extremely hard and who really enjoyed all the guys in the league and walked as a man of God. I know at times on the field there are frustration and emotions, but I feel I'm one of the easygoing guys on the field, although sometimes something can get under my skin. I'd like to be remembered as one of the better guys at his position and one who had a good testimony as a Christian.

Q: *What kinds of pressures do players in the NFL face?*
Brent: I think there's a lot of pressure being a professional athlete. Everyone has tremendous expectations of you and the way you treat people. They have to realize that we are just people who are playing a game. We are not any different, no matter what people make us out to be. I know there's a lot written about athletes and their making all this money, but I see the regular side of these guys as well.

It's a fast lifestyle for those who aren't Christians. The things that you see in everyday life are accelerated at an unbelievable level, and sometimes guys get caught up in it. We've seen it all. The money, the drugs, the women, and all the things that are out there for some of these young guys. I think it's tough to see guys go through this, thinking they can handle everything.

. . . I've tried not to change much the kind of person I am.

Q: *What is your favorite Bible passage?*
Brent: Proverbs 3:5–6: "Trust in the Lord with all your heart and lean not on your own understanding; in all your ways acknowledge him, and he will make your paths straight."

Q: *What kinds of people-helping ministries do you like to be involved in?*
Brent: We've been involved to a pretty good degree with City Team Ministries. They are working with unwed mothers. They have a big-time recovery program for men—sharing the gospel and getting them back on their feet with a job. They're working with needy families.

Also, I like to work with Young Life, because that's where I accepted Jesus. I have a golf tournament for Young Life. It's been raising money for that group for about five years. We've had all the 49ers help. We've been able to make a tremendous amount of money toward their budget.

Q: *How has your wife, Dana, helped you the most during your career?*
Brent: She's always been the encourager, especially when things are down. Men tend to internalize stuff. When things are going badly, we just try to fight it and tough it through. And she has always been there as my biggest supporter. The biggest thing is knowing that whether football worked or not or no matter where we were, she was always 100 percent behind me, encouraging me in my faith and in our marriage.

Guy McIntyre
A Great Guy

VITAL STATISTICS

Born February 17, 1961, in Thomasville, Georgia
6 feet 3, 290 pounds
College: University of Georgia
Position: Offensive Guard
1996 team: Philadelphia Eagles

CAREER HIGHLIGHTS

- Selected to five straight Pro Bowl teams (1989–1993)
- Played in three Super Bowls (1985, 1989, 1990) and won all three
- Named second-team college All-American (1983)

WARMING UP

Guy McIntyre toils in that relatively obscure world of offensive linemen. He has a national championship ring and three Super Bowl rings, but if someone were to ask you his uniform number or what teams he has played for in his NFL career, you might not be able to answer.

Guy McIntyre has protected Joe Montana. He's blocked for Brett Favre. He has kept defenders from tackling Herschel Walker. But what else do you really know about him?

It's high time you found out.

Guy McIntyre

magine how frustrating it must be to be an offensive lineman. You lift weights. You do the running. You sweat out the training camp just like everyone else. Then you go through the whole season and no one pays attention to you.

Look at the covers of sports magazines. Quarterbacks. Running backs. Tight ends. Wide receivers. Rarely do you see an offensive lineman.

As an offensive guard or tackle, a player just blocks. He gets knocked around. He lines up. Blocks. Gets knocked around. Blocks some more. Play after play after play.

He acquires no statistics: When was the last time you saw that someone was leading his team in blocking? He scores no points: even the rules are against him. He's not allowed to catch a pass even if the quarterback throws it to him.

Guy McIntyre toils in that relatively obscure world of offensive linemen. He has a national championship ring and three Super Bowl rings, but if someone were to ask you his uniform number or what team he has played for in his NFL career, you might not be able to answer.

He played in five straight Pro Bowls, has been a first-team All-Pro, and in college was the top offensive lineman in the Southeastern Conference. Yet many fans don't know as much about him as they know about their favorite team's trainer.

Guy McIntyre has protected Joe Montana. He's blocked for Brett

Favre. He has kept defenders from tackling Herschel Walker. But what else do you really know about him?

It's high time you found out.

After all, the talented Mr. McIntyre has even carried the ball on offense on at least three occasions in his career.

The first time he was in a position to grab leather was in high school in Thomasville, Georgia. In this community of 9,000 people, McIntyre was quite a successful tight end.

Down the road at another Thomasville high school, Charlie Ward prepped before he would be tabbed to lead Florida State to a national championship and win the Heisman Trophy along the way. McIntyre knew the Ward family. "Charlie's dad was a coach in the county school [and was even] a classmate of my mother when they were in school."

Two players from Thomasville. One not as well-known as the other but who has carved out an all-pro NFL career spanning twelve years; the other extremely well known but unable to hook on in the NFL. It just goes to show that high name recognition doesn't always tell the whole story.

While playing tight end and trying to make his way through high school, Guy McIntyre came face-to-face with a coach who gave the kid from a one-parent home the challenge he needed to avoid throwing away his life.

One day McIntyre showed up drunk at an intrasquad game. Fortunately for McIntyre, someone cared enough to confront him. It was Coach James Bryan.

"He called me into his office after the game," McIntyre recalls, "and read me my rights and everything. The next day at practice, I can remember it was hot and I was laying out in the sun, and we were stretching and stuff. I kind of had my eyes closed, but I could feel his presence come over me, and I could hear that voice. He said, 'McIntyre, what are you going to do with you life? Your daddy was a good football player. What are you going to do?' I didn't say anything, but it stuck in my mind. After that, I was pretty straight."

Straight enough to win a scholarship to the University of Georgia. It wasn't his first choice, but he chose it for the right reasons. "The place I wanted to go was USC," McIntyre says. "I used to see the Trojans on TV all the time. I had the opportunity to go, but it kind of faded out. I figured that California is 3,000 miles away. I started thinking about my mom. Ever since junior high she had watched me play every chance she could get. She worked a lot, but when I started going to high school and playing at night, she was always going to the games, and supporting me in basketball and football. I wanted to be close to her. That way, she could come and watch me play now and then."

McIntyre came on the scene at Georgia at about the same time the Bulldogs were rising to national prominence behind Herschel Walker. But although McIntyre had been recruited as a tight end, he was switched to the offensive line after a redshirt freshman year. As Walker's amazing skills would bring a national spotlight on the Bulldogs, McIntyre's new position put him in the shadows. He worked along the lines, protecting Walker and quarterback Buck Belue, in exchange for his national championship ring (1980) and a shot at the NFL.

Yet playing for a number one team bound for a national championship had its dividends for an offensive lineman. McIntyre describes the championship season as "a real exciting time to be there and to play." The Bulldogs were on TV every two or three weeks, he estimates. As a result, he ended up getting the TV time without going all the way to L.A.

McIntyre's time at Georgia also brought him face-to-face with a roommate who challenged his thinking. The roomie's name was Keith Hall, and he was a walk-on player for Vince Dooley's Bulldogs. He got on the team, McIntyre remembers, because "he worked very hard. He was a great example of someone who took what God gave him and gave it his best, and he won a scholarship for the last two or three years. Every day he gave everything."

And he gave Guy a lot to think about. "I was a freshman. I went to a school that had more people on campus than I had in the whole town" of Thomasville, he recalls. "And I was looking forward to the parties and stuff like that. But Keith, I always used to see him praying. Sometimes he used to fall asleep on his knees praying. He was a real nice guy, from south Georgia. One day he said, 'Guy, I want to talk to you.' He said, 'God loves you. You may not be ready, but He still loves you.'

"He was just a real loving, caring guy. If he had something, he'd give it to you. If you needed to borrow his car, he'd let you do it. He was right there for you. He was a great guy, a real example of what a Christian is supposed to be. He had his own little problems he used to fight, but he handled them through prayer. I really thank him for allowing me to share in it."

Yet throughout McIntyre's college years, he never came to the point at which he wanted to trust Jesus Christ. "I told Keith I really wasn't ready. I wanted to do the college scene."

It wasn't the college scene, however, that nearly did Guy McIntyre in. It was the NFL training camp scene and his overzealous play as a rookie. McIntyre went directly from Georgia and its shiny national championship to San Francisco, who the year before had just missed making it to the Super Bowl. When he came on the scene in 1984, he joined such 49er greats as Joe Montana and Dwight Clark, with Jerry Rice still to come.

"It was a great team—a great group of guys who had a lot of vision. They knew what they wanted to accomplish, and I was glad to be a part of it. I was just hoping I could make the roster. It was a real big challenge."

As a third-round pick, McIntyre was in fairly good shape, and he was encouraged that some of the 49ers themselves told him he'd make the team. But he was not about to take anything for granted.

"I went out like it was the end of the world," he says of that camp in 1984. "I was hitting anything that moved. During one practice I was blocking and really trying my hardest. I hit a guy named Jeff Stover, who at the time was a sort of project for Coach Bill Walsh. I hit him so hard I knocked him out. Bill went off on me like I hurt this guy, and the team's chances of winning were ruined. I was kind of scared to do anything anymore."

McIntyre obviously got over the shock of hurting the team's designated project and Walsh got over his anger; Guy went on to make the squad. During his first year in a 49er uniform, he saw action in all sixteen regular season games as a reserve guard, proving his worth and marking his time until he would get that coveted starter's role in the NFL.

When the playoffs rolled around that season, though, Guy McIntyre got his second career opportunity to get involved in the offense as something other than a blocker for the money guys.

As the season was winding down, Bill Walsh had a brainstorm, and it ended up hovering over Guy McIntyre's head. Walsh, who prides himself in his sometimes unusual offensive patterns, decided he wanted to employ a fullback in his backfield—a blocking back. Someone big and strong to give his true running back some protection. Someone even bigger than fullback Craig James.

Someone like guard Guy McIntyre—all 271 pounds of him. For the second time in his football life McIntyre would have a chance to touch the ball—this time in the NFC championship game in early January against the Chicago Bears. In the third quarter, Walsh called the play—a play in which an offensive lineman actually lines up in a position where he could possibly, conceivably, get the football.

First, though, McIntyre had to do something he had never done before. He had to bring the play into the huddle from the bench.

"The coach gave me the play," McIntyre recalls about this rookie-season highlight, "and I was trying not to forget the play, because I hadn't carried in plays before. I was running out onto the field, all excited. Joe Montana was sort of walking toward me to get the play. In my excitement, I kind of stepped on his foot really hard. He pushed me back, and I thought I had broken his foot. I thought we were going to lose the game.

"I didn't know if he was going to be able to go through with the play or not."

Not one to let a stepped-on foot fell him, Montana proceeded with the play, and McIntyre served as Wendell Tyler's blocking back. Tyler rambled ahead for 8 yards, and soon the 49ers had a field goal.

On the next series of downs, the Niners tried the Big Guy alignment again, this time with the McIntyre-created hole allowing Tyler to plow over from the 9 yard line for a 49er touchdown. When the game was over and the trick plays had all been stashed away, San Francisco had won 23–0 and was headed for a showdown with the Miami Dolphins in Super Bowl XIX.

Playing in a Super Bowl is a dream experience for any rookie, but for an offensive lineman to actually feel the leather in his hands with the opportunity to advance it must be the ultimate. Except when the handle is lost, which is exactly what happened when Guy McIntyre picked up the ball with less than one minute left in the first half.

The 49ers were leading 28–13, Miami had just scored a field goal, and just 12 seconds remained in the half. Uwe Von Schamann bounced a kick to the Niners' defenders, hoping to avoid a long kickoff return. The ball bounded right into the waiting arms of Guy McIntyre, who was playing special teams. Once again, the offensive guard had become the ball carrier. New to this whole concept of having the ball, McIntyre had a tough time deciding what to do.

First, he tried to down the ball by kneeling, but realized that he couldn't do that. "I kind of heard the whole stadium saying, 'Get up! Get up!' I went to get up and some guy hit me and knocked the ball out of my arms."

It was Joe Carter of Miami, a fellow rookie. The Dolphins recovered and kicked a field goal to cut the margin to 28–16 at the half.

For McIntyre, it was a dream that had turned into a nightmare.

"In the back of my mind I was thinking, *Man, if we lose this game by 3 points, I'm just going to be run out of the state.*"

As the team rumbled into the locker room at halftime, veteran Niner Jack "Hacksaw" Reynolds pulled up alongside McIntyre and assured him, saying, "Hey, Guy, don't worry about it, man. You've done a lot for this team. Don't worry about it."

"It made me feel good," McIntyre recalls. "He was a veteran, and he knew I was scared. It just helped me to keep my confidence up."

The Niners went on to win the game 38–16, so McIntyre didn't have to worry about being run out of town. Maybe not yet a great guy with his football exploits, but, hey, he had won a Super Bowl and was even a blocking back on offense! He was ready to catch a severe case of the fame-and-big-money blues. Like many pro athletes, McIntyre would catch the arrogant, nothing-can-stop-me-now attitude.

For McIntyre, it came on so fast and so furious that it could have derailed a promising career.

Small-town boy makes good. Plays in Super Bowl. Everybody knows him. He's got the big bucks now. He's got the car, a new Mercedes. Which way will he turn? Will he come home as the hero, ready to pitch in and help the community, or will he come home as the macho football jock, ready to remind anyone who will listen how important he is.

"A whole lot of stuff came on me at one time," says McIntyre, looking back on those post-rookie-year days. "I really didn't know how to handle it because I didn't have anybody to tell me what to do with the money, or how to manage it. My agent wasn't a very good agent. I just didn't have anybody I could turn to in my life at that time to give me real leadership in that area.

"I was twenty-three years old or so, driving around in a new Mercedes, with all kinds of money to spend. I just went out and partied— doing whatever—drugs, cocaine, and just living the life. It came time for me to start working out and getting ready for another season. People were talking about me."

Then an older woman, a friend of his grandmother, called Guy over to her house one day. She was nice, she was polite, but she was firm. "Baby, you know people are talking about you. They're saying this and that about you."

Guy knew she was right. "I took that to heart, because she didn't have to do it. My mother was concerned, but I wouldn't listen to her. She was real afraid of what was going on. It was obvious because I was in a small town, and everybody knew I was doing drugs, and doing it at a real high pace."

That didn't stop Guy's excesses right away. But it made him think. Then one day, walking by a bedroom mirror, he knew the truth. "I looked at myself, and I was weighing about 240 pounds. I had been out all night doing drugs. I kind of walked by a mirror in my room. It was dark and nobody was there, and I started to thinking about what was going on in my life. It was like I saw the man in the mirror, and I said to myself, *You're about to blow away everything that you ever worked for in your life and for what reason? Drugs.*

"I finally realized I was hooked, that I needed some help. I was down and didn't know where to turn, and I had always heard people talk about God and how He can change your life and how He can help you. I needed that help because I knew I couldn't stop doing what I was doing and I needed somebody to give me the courage to just admit I had a problem.

"That's what I asked God for that night. I laid everything on the line.

"God, I don't know if I'll ever play football again, but I need You to help me," McIntyre prayed. "And if I don't, it's my fault. I did it. It's not Your fault, it's something I did, but I know if I'm ever going to do anything again, be anybody, that I need You to help me to admit I have this problem."

And then McIntyre remembered one great guy, his college buddy Keith Hall. "I remembered him telling me about asking God into my life. That came across my mind. I had gone to church as a child, had believed in God, but I had never made a commitment to Jesus Christ. That night I did that. I asked God to help me. I trusted in Jesus."

Hall's prayers for his college friend had been answered, as had those of McIntyre's mother. She had taken her son to church several times as a child, but he hadn't wanted much to do with her religion. But she had remained faithful in prayer and church attendance as her boy grew. Now her born-again son had a call to make.

"I called some people in California, and I told them that I had the problem. Shortly after that, when it was time for me to go to camp, they took me on, and I went into rehab.

"From that time, I trusted in God. I put my career in His hands. I didn't know what was going to happen, I didn't know if the Niners would say, 'Well, we'll help you get over this problem, but we don't want you on our team.' I didn't know. I gave it all to Him. I put my career and everything in God's hand. He helped me through it."

The Niners stuck with their man, and he gave them just the kind of career they expected of him in repayment. During his second season, McIntyre hadn't yet become a full-time starter, but he did score his first NFL touchdown. Playing on the punt return team, he recovered a mishandled snap in the end zone in an October 20, 1985, game against the Lions. Finally, the guy who had worked in obscurity had been favored with a touchdown.

The offense just kept coming from big number 62. In 1988, he was asked to do something he hadn't done for almost ten years: line up at tight end. Just as he had been in high school and during his redshirt freshman year at Georgia, McIntyre was once more an eligible receiver. On September 18, he caught a 17-yard touchdown pass, the first reception and second touchdown of his pro career.

That pretty much concluded McIntyre's career as an offensive threat, but soon he was being mentioned as one of the best offensive linemen in the game. In 1989, he made the Pro Bowl for the first of five consecutive years, and was selected as an All-Pro. Between 1989 and 1993, McIntyre played in five Pro Bowl games, was All-NFC four times, started seventy-seven straight games, and played in his third Super Bowl. When it came to linemen, McIntyre had become a great guy, a dependable, if still not well-known, offensive guard.

After ten years in San Francisco's Candlestick Park and three Super Bowl rings, McIntyre decided to sign as an unrestricted free agent with the Green Bay Packers, a team he felt could take the next step into the Super Bowl.

The move would lead him to new friends, new challenges, and something he hadn't experienced in a long time—missing a football game. One of those new friends was Ken Ruettgers, a fellow offensive lineman and a strong brother in Jesus Christ. Ruettgers and his wife, Sheryl, made an immediate hit with the McIntyre household.

Guy and Michelle, along with their three children, Dejon, Mallory, and Ariel, were firmly settled into their home in Fremont, California. The move to Green Bay would mean that Michelle would have to take care of a ton of details in order to set up housekeeping. In order to help Guy and Michelle, Sheryl Ruettgers put together a care package of kitchen utensils to get the McIntyres started in their new digs. And Ken, who is not especially fond of animals in the house, agreed to watch Guy's dog. But the friendship went beyond pie pans and pooches.

In Green Bay, Ruettgers and McIntyre commuted back and forth to practice, getting to know each other, sharing their love for Jesus Christ, and discussing the differences in how Ruettgers, who is white, and McIntyre, who is African-American, view things. "We've grown really close in our relationships," McIntyre says about the friendship that became long-distance in 1995 when Guy moved on to Philadelphia. "We helped each other in several different areas of our lives."

McIntyre and the Packers took a step closer to the goal of returning to the Super Bowl by making it to the playoffs. But they had a sour taste in January 1995, when the Dallas Cowboys blew them out 35–9.

For a man who had become accustomed to winning, as McIntyre is, it must have been especially painful. And to add to the suffering, his old team, the 49ers, won the whole enchilada for the fourth time. Had he stayed in the Bay Area, he would have joined an elite group with four rings.

Yet McIntyre's twelve years in the league had matured his perspective. He knew how to win like a man, and he knew how to lose like a champion. "There's definitely a grieving period," he said after the loss. "You put a lot into it, and it hurts when you lose. But you go on with it. You go on with life because you know there's more to life than this game. The game allows you to do a lot of things, but it's not the totality of your life, and it shouldn't be.

"Whether I win or lose, I still know that God loves me and that He doesn't worry about me winning or losing football games. He just wants me to live my life like He designed for me to live it. Therefore, I can get over these things a little easier than those who don't have that relationship with Christ in their life."

That attitude sustained him in Green Bay during his first serious injury—one that not only kept him out of the lineup for the first time in years, but one that was potentially life-threatening. After the Packers' September 4 game against the Vikings, doctors discovered that McIntyre had a blood clot in his right calf.

In what appeared at first to be a simple bruise, the examiners found a clot that they thought might keep him out of the lineup for six months. Yet by October 20 he was cleared to play. He again saw action on October 31 against the Bears. The situation, which McIntyre calls "pretty scary," was over, and he was on his way to helping Green Bay in their quest.

Despite the good things that happened in Green Bay, McIntyre stayed but one year in the Wisconsin city. Just before the 1995 season began, he signed with the Philadelphia Eagles. Many factors enter a decision to switch teams. For McIntyre, the prospect of increased playing time was too good to pass up. Even more so than ever, McIntyre's value as a veteran was utilized by the coaches in Philadelphia. New coach Ray Rhodes did not hesitate to have his young coaching staff seek the advice of a man like McIntyre. "We had a young, first-year offensive line coach," McIntyre explained. "And he looks to us for advice on various things. I'm a little bit of a coach with some of the younger players. It helps to do that, because it makes you aware of new things."

Ironically, when McIntyre went to another young team looking for its chance at the Super Bowl, he went to a team that would lose the 1995 divisional playoffs to the Dallas Cowboys. Just as had happened the year before, the Cowboys shut the door on Guy McIntyre's title hopes, now as a Philadelphia Eagle.

The Philadelphia story for McIntyre did not have the same family tie-in as did the one in Green Bay, however. For the 1995 season, Guy had to tackle life alone. Michelle and the kids remained in Fremont, California, for schooling and other matters of consistency. "Green Bay is small and it's easy to move around," McIntyre explains. "But coming to Philly late in preseason and not really knowing what was going to happen, it was easier for me to get a little apartment and not worry about getting the family back and forth. All three of my kids go to the same school, so it was easier to let them stay home."

The great Guy that he is, McIntyre burned up the telephone lines talking to Michelle in the fall of 1995. He tried to work in visits to their California home whenever the Eagles' schedule permitted.

Guy McIntyre's family is very important to him. It comes across when he talks about how hard it is to keep a transcontinental relationship going with the kids by phone. And it comes across when he talks about how special his time with his kids was during this season of separation.

"When I was home, my kids clung to me," he says. "I have two young girls, and everywhere I went, they wanted to hold me or wanted me to hold their hand. Whenever I sat down, they were right there. I talked to them [by phone] just about every day."

Of course Mallory and Ariel like their daddy. That's natural. But it's also natural for others to like this big, strong offensive lineman. He has an easy laugh, and an engaging, low-key way of talking. He's not impressed with Guy McIntyre the football player, and he doesn't relish the limelight and fame that come even to guys who just block for a living.

"The worst part of being a pro football player," he says, "is the position people put you in—as far as being looked at as heroes. People put you in really hard positions sometimes, and you don't really know who to trust. For Christian guys, you can put that into perspective and make the situation work for God."

You may not have read too much about Guy McIntyre when you read accounts of the Eagles' incredible run in 1995, the Packers' playoff try of 1994, or even the 49ers' several Super Bowl wins. You won't see his name in stats reports, and you won't see many advertisers begging him to pitch their products. He has about as many points in the NFL as years played, and many football fans couldn't identify him.

But you get the impression that doesn't matter to him anymore. The days of the fancy Mercedes and hanging out flashing his money have given way to days of fancying Michelle and hanging out with three kids named Dejon, Mallory, and Ariel. He's quite a guy.

Q & A WITH GUY McINTYRE

Q: *Do you see any contradiction between being a Christian and playing a hard-hitting sport?*
Guy: God gave me the ability to do this, and as long as I do it in His glory, I think I'm OK. I'm not out there to hurt anybody. I'm out there to play within the rules of the game. I use the game to be a witness for Him.

Q: *When you leave the game, how do you want to be remembered?*
Guy: As a guy who played hard on the field, did all he could to help his teammates to win, lived a good life off the field, was a good person—a person you wouldn't mind having for a friend.

Q: *What do you do during the season to stay spiritually sharp?*
Guy: I go to team Bible studies. I try to make it a habit to read the Bible and pray each day. When I catch myself not doing that, I try to discipline myself to do it early in the morning.

Q: *What difference has your faith in Jesus Christ made in your life?*
Guy: It saved my life. God helped me have the courage to admit that I had a problem [drugs]. And He allowed whatever had to come after to come after. I was blessed with being able to continue to play. I kind of left it in God's hands, but I knew I needed to get that taken care of. My faith has given me the strength over the years to deal with adversities that have come into my life.

Also, it has changed my family life. It makes me enjoy my family a lot more—the time that I have to spend with them. It enriches me all of the time. With all of the craziness that I do here, my secret little haven is my family. It's helped my relationship with my wife. Just trying to deal with the day-to-day problems that arise within a family.

My faith has given me a lot of direction. It's given me a lot of peace.

Bryce Paup
Saying It with Power

VITAL STATISTICS

Born February 29, 1968, in Jefferson, Iowa
6 feet 5, 247 pounds
College: Northern Iowa
Position: Linebacker
1996 team: Buffalo Bills

CAREER HIGHLIGHTS

- Selected twice to Pro Bowl (1994, 1995)
- Led NFL in sacks with 17.5 (1995)
- NFC Defensive Player of the Month (November 1994)
- Selected third-team college All-American (1989)

WARMING UP

The pride problem that nagged him during his rookie year with the Packers came back after a strong second season. "I got a big head," Paup says. Pride would remain an issue during his third and fourth Packer seasons, even though a new coaching staff in 1992 should have made him aware that he was expendable.

He was about to learn about who ruled his football life—God or Bryce Paup.

Bryce Paup

On November 11, 1995, the National Football League fined Bryce Paup of the Buffalo Bills $12,000 for tackling a quarterback. That's like the IRS fining one of its auditors for finding a tax cheat. Or like ABC fining Sam Donaldson for digging up some dirt on a crooked politician. Or the Catholic church fining Mother Teresa for helping a poor person get medicine.

There are dirty football players in the NFL. There are obnoxious football players in the NFL. There are star-studded, gold-chained, self-centered glory grabbers in the NFL. There are cheap shot artists, camera muggers, and kill-the-quarterback thugs.

And then there are guys like Buffalo's Bryce Paup, who is none of the above. All Paup has done is quietly and without fanfare transform a Division 1-AA football career at Northern Iowa into an NFL career that has made him one of the best linebackers in the league.

And he has done so in an unobtrusive, Iowa farm boy kind of a way.

Yet there he was in early November 1995, labeled by the NFL as a bad-hit artist. To Paup, it was a difficult situation to be in during an otherwise stellar season.

In March of 1995, he had signed a three-year contract with the Bills, leaving the Green Bay Packers, with whom he had spent five seasons. Leaving Green Bay also was difficult. In fact, Paup calls it "the biggest struggle so far in my career. I had always thought I would stay in Green Bay my whole career."

It was in Green Bay that Paup had come into his own as a defender—an aggressive but fair defender. He had consistently improved his game each year he had played in Wisconsin.

In his rookie season with the Pack, Paup spent most of the year on the injured reserve list, recovering from a preseason hand injury. Although he played in just five games, he showed flashes of future glory as a special teams player.

Coming out of a Division 1-AA school as Paup did, he might be expected to start slow in the NFL. Paup, however, feels that the adjustment to the big time was not as difficult for him as it was for others, thanks to the defense played at Northern Iowa.

"The defense we ran [at NIU] was the same one that Green Bay ran, the terminology and everything," Bryce reveals. "It was just a matter of getting used to the bigger, quicker players. And getting used to the speed of the game and being technique-sound every play. Here, everybody is a great athlete, and you can't just get by with athletic ability like you did sometimes in college."

In addition to having played a Packer-type defense in college, Paup also found the transition from college to the pros a little easier due to one of his Packer teammates.

"Inside linebacker Brian Noble was a big help. He took me under his wing."

And it wasn't just with football that he helped the rookie. "I remember the first thing he said to me about the financial side of things. He said, 'It's not what you can afford. It's what you can save that counts.'

"On the field he would just tell me different things. He would make a play and I would say, 'Wow, how did you do that and why did you do this?'

"He would say, 'I read the running back or I read the guard.' He would tell me in certain formations who to read and key on."

With help from Noble and others, Paup was on his way to NFL success. Yet there were some big hurdles for the young linebacker to cross in his first years in Green Bay, not the least of which was a problem with pride.

"My first goal was just to make the team, and I thought everything was wrapped up in making the team. I took a lot of pride in making the team and when I did it, it was kind of an ego trip for me."

During his second year with the Packers, he began showing the strength and quickness and uncanny knack for pursuit that he is so well known for now. And he did so while playing a new position—the Packers' rover linebacker position. As he danced around the line, looking for an avenue to the quarterback, he often found the right route; he recorded 7½ sacks in his sophomore season.

On September 15 of his second year in the league, he served notice to the NFL that he had arrived when he recorded 4.5 sacks and 7 solo tackles against the Buccaneers. For his efforts, he was named the NFC's Co-defensive Player of the Week.

Two months later, he encountered a very bittersweet day. On November 17, at eight o'clock in the morning, his wife, Denise, gave birth to their first child, Alex. That was the good news. And then in the afternoon came the bad news. During a game that day, Bryce suffered a muscle tear in his left leg and was hobbled the rest of the season.

In spite of the injury, the pride problem that nagged him during his rookie year with the Packers came back after a strong second season. "I got a big head," Paup says. Pride would remain an issue during his third and fourth Packer seasons, even though a new coaching staff in 1992 should have made him aware that he was expendable.

"I was holding out at training camp when the guy who was in the starting position they wanted me to play was cut. It kind of made me think, *Wow, these guys aren't fooling around.*

"I came in late from holding out, and they threw me into a new position, and I was nervous about it. I didn't really perform that well because I'd never played there. It was a new coaching and defensive staff, and I didn't know what to expect.

"I was really nervous. I didn't know what was expected of that position, and I didn't know how to play it. I was too worried about the plays I'd made last year, and I thought I was supposed to make those plays, but that was totally out of the job description.

"I got myself all worked up about not making the same plays, and it hurt me because I was overaggressive, and you can't be aggressive when playing the position I was playing.

"About six weeks into the season, things weren't going well. The coaches decided it wasn't working out, and they decided to remove me from starting lineup."

He was about to learn about who ruled his football life—God or Bryce Paup. "I had been debating whether to give God football. I didn't want to do it because I'd always heard about people giving things to Him, and they were taken away. I didn't want that to happen.

"That's when I gave God football because I messed it up myself. If I hadn't given it to Him, it would have been taken away. After I'd prayed about that and decided, 'OK, if You want me to play football anymore, then You've got to help me and turn this around,' it seems from that point on I had success in the season. I got 6 ½ sacks in the last ten games. From that point on my season turned around, and I was productive and I had a lot more peace about the situation."

In 1993, Paup's third year in Green Bay, the coaches moved him again. "I played four different positions and had a lot of success. Tony Bennett held out that training camp and I was starting at his position, a position that I didn't have a lot of experience at, but knew how to play. I had 8 ½ sacks in the first eight ball games, and I was sharing the lead on the team for sacks.

"When Tony came back, I got hurt. The coaches decided to move me to still another position when I could play."

Paup was a bit confused. He had the statistics, and he seemed to be productive, yet he still didn't think he had the confidence of the coaching staff. Yet he knew that even the coaches didn't have ultimate control over his life and career.

"They weren't counting on me; they didn't think I could do the job. It was their perception, but you can't count on what they think, because God had control over it. No matter how hard they tried messing with me, or changing me, God said He was in control. He had the final say in it, and they didn't."

Despite the frustrations he was encountering, Paup was still sure he had done the right thing in giving football to God. "I had tried it my way and it didn't work, and there was no sense of going back to my way. Even sometimes when I questioned what was going on, I knew He was in control. He always came back and made everything work out when I didn't think it was going to."

To Paup, the principle of letting God control his situation came straight out of the Bible. "'To whom much is given, much is required.'" he says, paraphrasing Luke 12:48. "God was the one who got me to that point, and I should do everything as unto Him and let Him have the glory."

By 1994, Paup emerged as one of the best defenders in football. It was a Pro Bowl year, one in which Paup started all sixteen regular season games, recorded 79 tackles, 7½ sacks, scored his first NFL touchdown on an interception of Lions' quarterback Scott Mitchell, and intercepted Bears' QB Erik Kramer twice in one game.

The Packers had become a team heading in the right direction, and Paup had begun to consider Green Bay his permanent home. So when his free-agency year rolled around and the Bills came calling for him in the spring of 1995, it had to be something other than the money Buffalo was offering him that swayed his thinking.

"I guess I got too comfortable in Green Bay. I wasn't sharing my testimony like I should," he says, speaking of his love for Jesus Christ. "Sometimes it takes you getting shaken up a little bit and getting out of your comfort zone before you can see the light and start witnessing again."

For Paup, the move east to Buffalo was a new beginning in more ways than just the one relating to football. With a new team, he felt he could be more vocal about his faith. "When I started out in Green Bay, I was the quiet, timid guy who wouldn't say much in the locker room. And even though I had strong Christians around me, I wouldn't pipe up. But when I got here to Buffalo, someone asked me a question at minicamp, and I started sharing the gospel with him. In Green Bay, I wouldn't have done that."

The gospel has always been important to Bryce Paup and the entire Paup family during his growing-up days back in Iowa. "We were in church all the time," he says. "We sat in the second row from the front, so we had to be good all the time. We had to pay attention because my mom would play the piano or the organ. Dad was in the back making tapes of the sermons."

The four Paup children heard the gospel weekly, and the message made an impact on Bryce early. At the age of four, he accepted Jesus Christ as his Savior.

But just as the old bumper sticker says, "Christians aren't perfect, just forgiven." Bryce showed his imperfection in a couple of different ways, and he had to come back to God a couple of different times.

In high school, Paup was the star on a very small football team. In fact, there were only sixteen players on Scranton High School's team. "I was good at football, and I was bigger than everyone else," says Paup of those days. That's not hard to imagine.

What is hard to imagine given Paup's personality and his image as a clean-living, respected athlete is that, as he says, "I started getting in trouble a little bit in high school. We basically ran out our shop teacher. Of course, now that I look back on it, I feel sorry for him. But we were relentless in getting after him."

Fortunately for Paup, there was someone in his school who was man enough to stand up to the big, raw-boned football player and read him the riot act. One day before parents' night during the football season the principal sat down the big sophomore and told him he could not play because of his behavior.

"Right then and there I decided to straighten out my act. I pleaded and begged with him, and he finally decided to let me play in the game. From that point on, I pretty much kept my nose clean."

Well, at least until his junior year. That's when his math teacher got him angry. The teacher "thought I had some potential in my classes," Bryce recalls. "One day I wasn't paying attention, and he just ripped into me in front of the class. It made me mad, and I wanted to show him that I could do better." But this was a constructive anger. Determined to show his teacher, Bryce made the honor roll the next year—twice.

The next year he also had a girlfriend named Denise. Bryce met her at a youth group lock-in just before his senior year started, after his cousin invited him to the event. Denise had already graduated from high school and was headed to Northern Iowa in the fall. And the two were already somewhat acquainted. In fact, Bryce's dad had done some work for Denise's dad a few years earlier. When Bryce was in the ninth grade, Denise's father had come home from work one day and told his daughters, "You girls ought to check out that Paup boy. He's a nice kid. A good-looking kid."

So now it was three years later, and the two were checking each other out. "I had kind of been praying for a nice girl I could meet and eventually marry," Paup says. "She was going out with another guy at the time, but things just worked out for us."

Soon the two were dating, and Denise was off to Northern Iowa. While there, she and a friend were out for pizza one night when the friend, who was a cheerleader, saw some of the UNI coaches. She walked over to them and told them about Denise's boyfriend. When they discovered how big Bryce was, the coaches nearly dropped their pizza.

Not many opportunities to play major college football come to the boys from small Iowa towns like Scranton, so when the UNI coaches came calling, Paup was more than willing to head for Cedar Falls.

During Paup's senior year at Scranton, right before he took off for Northern Iowa, he "made a recommitment to God." For the first two and a half years of his college life, he lived by that commitment to the Lord. But then as so often happens with athletes who begin to succeed, he drifted away. "I started to become a good football player, and I started to rebel a little bit. Some of the NFL scouts coming through were asking the coach about me, and I was starting to think, *Hey, I have a shot.*"

School friends, including some teammates, invited Bryce to parties, and soon he thought, *Maybe I'm missing out on something.* So he began going out Friday and Saturday nights. But before he got too wrapped up in the party scene, he came to his senses.

"I thought I was having a good time, but it hurt my performance on the field and in the classroom. I decided it wasn't worth it, because I only had one more year, and if I wanted to make the NFL, I had to get my act together."

He also noticed that there was a difference between him and his teammates. They could party and not seem to be affected by it on the field, but these "extracurricular activities" were bringing him down. Finally, Paup saw why. "Some of those guys didn't care about football. They were just going through the motions half the time. It didn't affect what they were doing on the field because they really didn't care."

But Paup did care, and he wanted to change.

So, once more, Bryce Paup got together with God and told Him that he wanted to follow Him. "I rededicated myself to being what God wanted me to be. I discovered during that time that God will never leave you. But sometimes you have to face the consequences that go along with your choices."

Besides getting together with God, Paup also met with his pastor, who prayed with Bryce. "He prayed me through it," the big man recalls. "After that, things turned around, and I've been on track since."

But what about Denise during this time? She knew that Bryce's party times in college were not God-honoring. Yet she stood by her man. "She stuck with me," Paup says now, with admiration. "She was a Christian. Even through the partying times and the good times I thought

I was having, she stuck with me. When I wanted to rebel, she was there to bring me back."

Spiritually, Paup was now ready to take on the NFL. Physically, he had proved his worth with an outstanding career at Northern Iowa. Among the highlights of his four years, which included a 1-AA playoff berth for the Panthers as a junior and an All-Gateway Conference selection as a senior, was his breakthrough game as a sophomore. "We went into Western Illinois, and they were expected to win the championship. But we came up with a big game. I had three sacks and three forced fumbles. We blew them out 52–0. After that, the scouts started taking notice."

When the scouts started calling, Paup could begin to feel his lifetime dream come true. "I had always dreamed of playing in the NFL. Ever since I can remember, people would ask me, 'What do you want to be when you grow up?' And I said I wanted to be a pro football player and play on TV."

First with the champions of Super Bowls I and II, the Packers, and then with the AFC champion Buffalo Bills, Paup played on TV and in America's great football stadiums. With the Bills in 1995 Paup would take his game to a new level.

"The Bills saw me in a different light," he says about that year. "They used my strengths instead of making me do things that I wasn't that good at." There would be no more shifting Paup around to new positions depending on who was hurt and who was running the defense. With Buffalo, Marv Levy and his defensive brain trust looked at Paup and installed him at outside linebacker. No more rover. No more middle linebacker.

Paup was free to bust loose. "I'm an attack-style player," he says, understating nicely what he does best.

Then came the Indianapolis game, the controversial tackle of quarterback Paul Justin, and a surprising new chapter in Bryce Paup's life. In that early November game against the Colts, Paup was an equal opportunity sacker, nailing each of the three Indy signal-callers who played that day. This gave him a league-leading 11 sacks on the year.

But the hit of Justin also gave him a peck of trouble. The NFL notified the Bills of the $12,000 fine for that hit, saying that Paup was being penalized for a "tackling technique." Paup's first response to the fine was no comment.

He had already spoken. After the game, he had said, "I didn't want to take him out of the game. I hope he's OK. As a defender, you look forward to plays like that. You want to rock their world. But you never want to hurt anyone."

Bills' general manager John Butler put the situation in perspective when he said, "Bryce Paup's one of the cleanest players in the league."

Paup recognizes what damage this kind of incident can do to his reputation, and he decided to stop the flow of negativism. The day after the NFL meted out its fine, Paup said he was planning to sue the NFL for defamation of character. He said the fine made him look like a dirty player.

But whatever the outcome, Paup is still clinging to his trust in God. "When you're serving God with all your might, Satan's going to try to get after you," Paup says, trying to answer why this would happen to him. "That was the way I think he thought he could get at me, and it did shake me up for about a week. That's all I could think about. I was really depressed. *Why are they picking on me?*

"But I started thinking about it. That can happen to anybody. And it wasn't a vicious hit. It was a hard hit, but that's what I got paid for. I did everything by the book. I had my head up. I didn't hit him head-to-head. I just figured, *Well, God knows my heart. He knows I wasn't trying to hurt him. He knows I wasn't trying to be cheap.*"

The difficulties surrounding the tackle of Paul Justin, though, could hardly take away the luster from Paup's finest season. He led the league in sacks with 17.5 and was named to the Pro Bowl.

While he was taking his game to new heights, he was also striving to keep his relationship with his wife, Denise, and their children, Alex and Nathan, his top priority. "I'm trying not to spend too much time on the job," says the man whose job goes far beyond those Sunday afternoon glamor hours on TV. It's lifting weights. It's watching film. It's studying. "I'm trying to get my priorities straight at home so I'm not studying film instead of playing with the kids or talking to my wife."

He's also striving to keep that pride factor from coming back into his life. "Something I didn't do that I've done in the past: I don't watch the news, I don't read the paper, I don't listen to the radio. You can't get proud if you aren't hearing what everyone is saying. If you don't hear them saying, 'You're so great' and all that stuff. I'm just listening to my coaches, and that has helped a lot."

And listening to God. "I'm trying to stay in the Word. I attend the

Bills' Bible study with our chaplain, Fred Raines. Also, my wife is in a Bible study with the Bills' wives, and we pray together. I read the Bible to the kids at home every morning."

Bryce Paup is a man of power. Power that comes from a body that he knows God has given him: "God gave me a talent and has blessed me in football." Power that comes from a faith that will take him through tough times: "I figure God will turn this around [the NFL fine] and make something good come out of it." Power that comes from a strong family that raised him right and prays for him. Power that comes to a man who loves his wife and children and makes them a high priority.

It's the power that can quench a man's pride and give him peace in the violent world of pro football.

Q & A WITH BRYCE PAUP

Q: *What would you say your biggest strength is?*
Bryce: When I set my mind to do something, there's no changing me. It doesn't matter what happens, how discouraged I get. If I set my mind to it, I'm going to see it through to the end. I got that from my parents. That's just the way they are. When they set their mind to do something, they work hard till they get it done.

Q: *What legacy do you want to leave in the NFL?*
Bryce: That I was a good person. That I gave it all I had on the field.

Q: *What's the downside of being in the NFL?*
Bryce: In the pros, everybody is telling you how good you are. If you don't stay in the the Word of God and stay focused, it can go to your head. That's when you might get knocked down a few notches. The biggest thing coming to Buffalo was that I had a great contract and had been to the Pro Bowl. My biggest prayer was, "Please don't let pride be a factor."

Q: *Who were the most influential people in your life as you were grow-ing up?*
Bryce: My dad and mom, just because they were always there. I respected them. They were good, hard-working people. They feared God, and they went to church all the time. They were just good, solid people. They always kept God first.

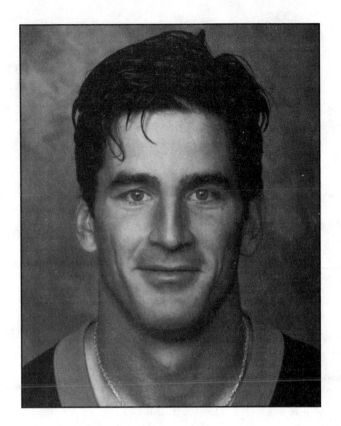

Frank Reich
Playing for a Song

VITAL STATISTICS

Born December 4, 1961, in Lebanon, Pennsylvania
6 feet 4, 210 pounds
College: Maryland
Position: Quarterback
1996 team: New York Jets

CAREER HIGHLIGHTS

- Played in four Super Bowls (1991, 1992, 1993, 1994)
- Directed the Bills to greatest comeback victory ever in NFL playoffs (1992)
- Won his first NFL start, 23–20, completing 57 percent of his passes for 214 yards and two touchdowns
- Completed 63.9 percent of his passes as a senior at Maryland (1984)

WARMING UP

N ow the Bills were staring at a scoreboard that read 35–3. They needed 33 points, but only 28 minutes remained in the game. Since they had scored just 6 points against the Oilers in the last 92 minutes, the math just wasn't on their side.

But Frank Reich was on their side. Frank Reich of the huge comeback at Maryland eight years earlier. There were a couple of other factors that Reich had in his favor. One was the attitude he had learned in that college comeback extravaganza. "We just said, 'Hey, let's take it one play at a time and one touchdown at a time.'"

Touchdown one came with just 8:25 left in the third quarter, and the Oilers still led 35–10. The second factor was the song. Over on the sidelines Reich was doing his best Orel Hershiser imitation. He was humming the song his sister had sent him earlier in the week, being reminded of the source of his strength.

"That song had been so ingrained in my mind that I couldn't get it off my mind." And soon Reich was on the mind of the Houston Oilers.

Frank Reich

Neither baseball's Orel Hershiser nor football's Frank Reich gets paid for singing. Those players get paid for how well they throw a ball and what decisions they make in doing so.

But both athletes have brought a lot of attention to specific songs they sang during vital athletic contests they were involved in.

Hershiser, if you remember, used the traditional church doxology as a comforting refrain as he sat in the dugout between innings during the final game of the 1988 World Series. Later, after the Dodgers had dispatched the A's and Hershiser had collected the Series MVP Award, he sang the song of praise for an admiring Johnny Carson on *The Tonight Show*. It may have been the most famous song in baseball since Dizzy Dean sang the "Wabash Cannonball."

For Reich, the singing quarterback, the song of choice was "In Christ Alone," and the dramatic circumstance was a game that has been billed the greatest comeback in NFL history. It was played on January 2, 1993, and it set the Bills up for their third straight Super Bowl appearance.

Ironically, Reich had dabbled in Hershiser's sport as a high school athlete, but left it in pursuit of a career in football.

It seemed the natural thing to do. After all, his dad, Frank Sr. (by the way, Orel's dad is named Orel Sr.), had set a pretty good pace as a college football player himself. The elder Reich was captain of the Penn State Nitanny Lions during the 1955 season. He played both quarterback and defense for Penn State. As a senior, he played in the East-West Shrine All-Star Game.

This was no Todd Marinovich story in which dad trains his son from day one to be a major college quarterback—at the cost of his childhood. No, Frank Reich's dad did not push him to play the sport.

"My dad never once said to me that he wanted me to play football or did anything to encourage me to play football," Frank says as he thinks back. "He would always say, 'If you want to play football, great, if you want to play in the band, great, whatever you want to do, we'll support you.'"

That in itself might not seem like a remarkable statement, but a story from young Frank's life proves how carefully his dad protected him from the pressure of trying to follow in his daddy's footsteps.

"I was ten years old," Reich recalls, "when one day, my mom and dad were out and I was snooping around in their room. I was in their closet and I found two big bags and pulled them out. They were scrapbooks from when my dad played at Penn State. They called him an unsung hero and told about an interception record he had and another for returns for a touchdown. The reports said he was captain of the team."

This was news to Frank. "My dad had never told me he was a good football player."

Reich also remembers his dad later letting him take an old football outside to play with. After he lost it, he found out it was a game ball his dad had received when he had intercepted a pass and returned it for a touchdown. "He never once said anything about it," Reich marvels.

And then there was Frank Sr.'s game jersey from the East-West Shrine All-Star game. "We'd wear it outside, and we never had any idea what it was," young Frank says. "It was just an old football jersey to us. I still have it to this day."

When Frank asked his dad why he never told him about his days as a star at University Park, his father said simply, "I never wanted you to feel like you had to play football just because I played football."

Yet play football young Frank did. First at Cedar Crest High School in Lebanon, Pennsylvania, where he was good enough to receive scholarship offers from the University of Maryland and Penn State, among others.

Which would he choose? A school in another state or the school all Pennsylvania kids dream of playing at—the school where his dad crafted a great career?

Surprisingly, Maryland won Frank's heart. "I never really considered going to Penn State," he says. "They came into the recruiting picture late, and I had already narrowed down my choices."

So off he went to be a Terp. And to become known as the engineer of the greatest comeback in NCAA history. At least, that's what many college observers call the Terp's surprise upset of the Miami Hurricances. Frank Reich was at the helm when his college team recorded the NCAA's greatest comeback victory in terms of overcoming a deficit. Eight years later as quarterback for the Buffalo Bills, Reich would lead the NFL club to what observers then called the greatest comeback in pro football history.

The college version of *Dead Men Walking* occurred on November 17, 1984. Reich was in his senior year of eligibility as the quarterback at Maryland, and the Terps were facing the mighty Miami Hurricanes, then 8–2. Playing on their home field, the Orange Bowl, the 'Canes'were blowing away Maryland, 31–0 at halftime.

Up to this point, Frank Reich had not seen any action. He had missed three games with a separated shoulder, but he was healthy enough to play if he was needed. Was he ever. At the half, the Maryland coach Bobby Ross—who would later take the San Diego Chargers to the Super Bowl—looked at Reich and said, "You'll be starting the second half."

With Reich at the wheel, Maryland put their game into high gear. At one time, the Terp offense ran off six straight touchdowns as Reich hit 12 of 15 passes for three TDs. And he ran the ball in for another score. By the time the stunned Orange Bowl crowd knew what hit them, Maryland was headed for the bus with a 42–40 victory. No college team had ever come back from a 31-point halftime deficit to win.

For Frank Reich, life at Maryland had other benefits beyond the obvious ones of crafting this comeback and completing a football career that would lead to his being drafted in the third round in 1985 by the Buffalo Bills.

It also marked the beginning of two exceptionally important relationships for him. One with a young woman he had known since sixth grade, and one with Jesus Christ.

Long before Frank went to Maryland, he had been friends with Linda Fick. In fact, he says that in high school, they were "best friends." But it was more like a sister-brother relationship than boyfriend-girlfriend. "Even when I was dating other girls," he says, "and she was dating other guys, we were best friends. I would tell her all my girl problems, and she would tell me all her boy problems."

· When Frank went off to University Park, Linda ventured to Lancaster, Pennsylvania, to attend Franklin & Marshall College. "I wasn't dating anybody, and she wasn't dating anybody, so I invited her to come down to a football game at Maryland," Reich recounts. "Linda came down to the game, and we went out on our first date after all those years.

"It's actually a funny story. I had so much respect for her, and her friendship was so valuable to me that I never would even dream of saying to her, 'Let's make this a date.' So we were going out to dinner with another couple just as friends, as we normally did. We were sitting in the back of the car. She leaned over to me and said to me, 'I want you to do me a favor.' She said, 'I want you to treat me like I'm a date.' And it just totally blew me away.

"So I treated her like she was a date, which really wasn't any differently, except that at the end of the night, I kissed her good night, and that was it. From there, probably six months after that, we started dating more seriously and got married about five years later."

The other relationship that began during Reich's college years was one that according to Frank was initiated 2,000 years ago. Soon after the big comeback win against Miami, Reich began to develop in earnest a relationship with Jesus Christ as his Savior. But in the telling of his salvation experience, he points to A.D. 30, not the 1980s.

"When Jesus died on the cross for my sins was when I was specifically saved," Reich begins. "I had a conversion experience when I was a senior in college, but I don't like to tell people that I got saved then. I know there's nothing wrong with it, but I really don't like to tell people I was saved when I was a senior in college. I usually tell people I was saved 2,000 years ago when Jesus died on the cross for my sins. Then I accepted that forgiveness when I was in college.

"The Bible says that no one comes to the Father unless He draws us, and I believe that He was drawing me from the time I was young, through the family I grew up in. When I was a senior in college was when I really truly started to hold on to what it was to have a relationship with Jesus Christ.

"It is truly by God's grace that I am saved. I don't want anyone to think that it was the saying of a prayer that saved a soul. I truly believe that only God regenerates. We're spiritually dead. Ephesians 2 says that we were dead in our trespasses and our sins, and God made us alive with Christ. He quickened our heart. And that was strictly by His grace. Had He not done that, I would be a lost sheep."

Clearly, Frank Reich has a passion for God. Grateful for the forgiveness he has in Jesus Christ, he is careful to present his salvation as God's working in his life—God's gift to him. As he talks about his relationship with Jesus, Frank Reich is quiet, serious, thoughtful. He chooses his words judiciously, for he understands he is dealing with a subject of eternal importance.

So much has happened to Reich in those intervening years since he put his faith in Jesus Christ while at Maryland. The marriage to Linda Fick (which, interestingly, rhymes with Reich). The birth of the Reiches' three children. The wild ride as a member of the Buffalo Bills, including another fantastic comeback on January 2, 1993. (More on that shortly.) He would play in four Super Bowls. Eventually he would be a successful quarterback with the expansion Carolina Cougars.

And through it all, Reich has continued to learn spiritual lessons. Some of the lessons mirror those his dad taught him back in Lebanon; some are new revelations, which have come to him through circumstances, people, and events. But of all the concepts and ideas that have colored Frank Reich's years as a pro football player, none seems to have made such an impact on him and on others than that mountaintop experience we can call Comeback II.

Let's set the scene a bit as we begin to examine why this single day has meant so much to a man whose pro career has spanned twelve football seasons.

For seven seasons, Frank Reich had dutifully backed up the Bills' star quarterback, Jim Kelly. In his first two seasons he played in a total of four games. During years three and four he played in zero and three games, respectively, attempting no passes. Then his involvement began to increase.

In his fifth season, he started three games and won them all, including a typical Reich outing in his first NFL start. Against the Rams he engineered a couple of fourth-quarter drives to lead the Bills to a come-from-behind win. For the year, he completed 53 of 87 passes.

During his sixth season his stats were down a bit, yet he still contributed to some important Bills' wins.

In 1991, Reich appeared in sixteen games, his most ever, and fired six touchdown passes.

Similar statistics in 1992 left no indication of what lay ahead for Reich in the postseason. But in the final game of the regular season, Jim Kelly was injured against the Houston Oilers. Reich knew he would be under center the next weekend for an AFC playoff rematch with Houston.

As he prepared for only his seventh starting assignment in eight years with Buffalo, Reich concentrated on two things: first, watching so much Oiler game film that offensive coordinator Tom Bresnahan finally suggested that Reich ease up a bit on the viewing, and second, spending a lot of time listening to a new song his sister had told him about.

The film-watching is pretty much standard procedure for NFL quarterbacks, but the song-monitoring added a bit of an unorthodox touch to Reich's prep time.

"My sister had called me and told me about this song," Reich explains about the tune that he would soon make famous. "It was called 'In Christ Alone,' and she told me it was a great song. She thought I would enjoy it. So I listened to it on Wednesday night for the first time. I was really moved by the song. Between that Wednesday night and Sunday game time, I listened to that song a hundred times."

Hundreds of times, Reich heard the singer describe "the source of strength" in every victory to be Christ alone.

With the Houston defense and the words to "In Christ Alone" occupying Reich's mind, he entered Buffalo's Rich Stadium to battle the Oilers. Still, things looked dark for the Bills as they began their quest for a third Super Bowl appearance. They were playing a team that had pasted them 27–3 in their last regular season game, and they were playing them without Jim Kelly.

By halftime, the darkness was palpable. The Bills were down 28–3. Their only hope seemed to be a quick start in the second half, a lightning score or two and some Houston mistakes. What they didn't need was a 58-yard interception return by Oiler safety Bubba McDowell. But that's what the Oilers gave them.

Now the Bills were staring up at a scoreboard that read 35–3. They needed 33 points, but only 28 minutes remained in the game. Since they had scored just 3 points against the Oilers in the last 92 minutes, the math just wasn't on their side.

Neither was the lineup. Besides not having Kelly, the Bills had lost running back Thurman Thomas, linebacker Cornelius Bennett, and defensive lineman Bruce Smith to injuries.

But Frank Reich was on their side. Frank Reich of the huge comeback at Maryland eight years earlier.

There was a difference this time, though. "I was partly responsible for getting behind by 32 points," he explains, recalling that he had not put Maryland in the hole. And surely that must play games with a quarterback's mind. Gun-shy might be one way to describe how he must have felt.

Yet there were a couple of other factors that Reich had in his favor. One was the attitude he had learned in that college comeback extravaganza. "We just said, 'Hey, let's just take it one play at a time and one touchdown at a time.'"

Touchdown one came on the next series of plays after McDowell's interception. It seemed harmless enough, though, for the Oilers still led 35–10 with just 8:25 left in the third quarter.

The second factor was the song. Over on the sidelines Reich was doing his best Orel Hershiser imitation. He was humming that song his sister had sent him earlier in the week, being reminded of the source of his strength.

"Each time we would come off the sideline, I was humming that song in my mind, over and over again," Reich recalls. "Obviously, I was thinking what we needed to do football-wise, but that song had been so ingrained in my mind that I couldn't get it off my mind."

And soon Reich was on the mind of the Houston Oilers.

The Bills executed a perfect onside kick, with the help of the Oilers' return unit, which retreated on the kickoff, allowing the Bills time to get downfield and snag the ball. Then Reich took over, firing a 38-yard, high-arching pass to Don Beebe for a touchdown. The score had narrowed to 35–17. Better, but the Bills still looked to be far out of the picture.

Their defense, though, stopped Houston cold, which gave Reich the ball back on Buffalo's own 41-yard line. In four plays, he had the Bills in the end zone again, this time on a pass to Andre Reed. Now the Bills were down by just 11, and there was still 4:21 left in the third quarter. "It was pretty amazing," Reich recalls. "At this point I really felt we had a legitimate chance to win the game." In just 4½ minutes, the

Bills had rattled off 21 points. The math was starting to look better.

Two minutes and 21 seconds later, the singing quarterback fired another pass to Reed and the Bills trailed just 35–31 as the third quarter ended.

The teams battled like two tired boxers through most of the fourth quarter, with neither team able to get the ball across the goal line or through the uprights. Finally, with just three minutes to go, Reich hit Reed for the touchdown that put the Bills ahead. They had scored 35 unanswered points and now led 38–35.

With just 12 seconds left, the Oilers' Al Del Greco nailed a 26-yard field goal to tie the game and send it into overtime. In the extra period, the Oilers got the ball first, but quarterback Warren Moon was intercepted, the Bills ran two plays to get into position, and Steve Christie booted a 32-yard field goal to win. The Bills, seemingly buried just 30 minutes earlier, were alive and kicking, on their way to the next round of the playoffs.

Frank Reich's reputation was solidified with this incredible January performance. In only his seventh start as an NFL quarterback, Reich had blazed his name on the consciousness of every fan in the land. With that reputation came some expectations.

For one, fans expected miracles to happen every time Frank Reich stepped on the field. And in a sense, Reich thought it might be happening as well. "When Jim Kelly got hurt in the second quarter of the Super Bowl, and I came in with us just a few points behind, I guess my first thought was, *This is gonna be a storybook finish, and I'm gonna have an opportunity to come in and play, and we're gonna win. And I'm gonna give the glory to God.*"

Problem was, it didn't happen that way. The Cowboys were just too good, and there would be no miracle this time. There would only be questions.

Running through Reich's mind after his team had been manhandled by Dallas 52–17 was this: *How could this happen?* As he sat back in his seat and endured the long flight from Los Angeles, he turned again to that song. The one he had hummed so faithfully on the day of the miracle comeback.

He put on his headset, inserted "In Christ Alone," and listened.

"At that time, those words took on a whole new meaning in my life," he contends. "All of a sudden, I realized that when it says, 'In every victory let it be said of me that my source of strength and my source of hope is Christ alone,' I began to see that the victory was a victory over the devastation and disappointment and the constant questioning of why for the rest of my life.

"I prayed, and I felt as if God gave me victory over that Super Bowl loss. I haven't looked back since."

Reich began to recognize that "God had other plans" than for him to be the hero that day.

God's plans for Reich also took another turn two years later when he signed a contract with the Carolina Panthers. After ten years of backing up Jim Kelly, Reich was about to get his shot at a starting job.

As Reich reported to training camp for the expansion Panthers, the consensus was that he would have to battle veteran Jack Trudeau for the starting position. Also in camp was Kerry Collins, from where else but Lebanon, Pennsylvania, and Penn State University, but he was a rookie who was given a slim chance to lead the team.

In the team's first-ever regular season game, Reich showed what he could do. Battling the Atlanta Falcons into overtime, the Panthers finally lost, 23–20. But Reich won the starting job, passing for 329 yards on the day.

The honeymoon, however, didn't last long. Soon Kerry Collins had vaulted past both veterans and assumed the starting role. It ended up being a difficult year for Reich as he found himself back in that unwanted and all-too-familiar role as backup.

Looking back on that first year, Reich knows that the disappointments he has endured cannot outweigh the lessons he has learned.

"It's definitely a lesson. I just wouldn't have thought this would have happened to me," Reich said. "But I know that it could. I know how sinful I am. The fact that I thought I had football under control, was the very thought that showed that I didn't.

"I look back on that now, thinking I had control on it when in actuality I need to give it up every day. Yet I'll never give up that desire. The desire is the same. The only thing that changes is the motivation. Now I'm playing and motivated and compelled not for the love of the starting position but by the love of Christ. Not to play for my own honor but for the honor of the Lord.

"I'm still working as hard as I can. Whatever happens, happens, but I'm going to try my best."

Whatever happens will happen with the New York Jets, for in spring 1996, Reich signed a two-year contract with the Jets. He was returning to the Empire State. Earlier in 1996 the Jets had acquired Neil O'Donnell from the Steelers, so again Reich would be backing up a Super Bowl quarterback.

The song has played in Frank Reich's ears hundreds of times, and each time it reminds him of a truth that he wants to keep on his mind. It remains his goal every time he steps onto the field in the Meadowlands.

Sure, there are the obvious goals of helping the team and leading them to victory, and he is careful to make sure everyone knows how important that is to him. But there is something else that happens when a man does his job for Christ alone.

"My desire is to serve Jesus on the football field, to show what it is to be a godly man on the football field and doing his best. When I step out on the field, I seek no greater honor than just to know Him more. As a result of serving Him on the football field—win or lose, good performance or bad—I want to know God more intimately. And I want to do that with every ounce of energy I have."

If that were to happen, the miracle would be clear to all who see it. And the glory would go to Christ alone. It's a song worth playing for.

Q & A WITH FRANK REICH

Q: *What is the best advice you would have for today's fathers?*
Frank: Model unconditional love. It is something that none of us have a handle on, but through the power of the Holy Spirit we're able to give some hope to this kind of love. Somehow, in humility and love, we need to let our children know that we love them just as much when they don't succeed in the world's eyes as when they do.

Q: *How do you stay sharp spiritually?*
Frank: I am involved with the team Bible study. Also, Linda and I have our own personal Bible study that we do. For instance, we will go through the book of Colossians together. In addition, one of the biblical principles that I've been taught is multiplication. I'm being discipled by someone, and I'm also discipling someone else. It's like a spring-fed lake. I'm being fed, but at the same time, I've got to let some out.

Q: *Did you face any major setbacks as a kid?*
Frank: (Reich paused a long time before answering, obviously because this was painful to discuss.) The very first time I tried alcohol, I got caught by the police and was suspended from school. That wasn't a pretty sight, because my mother was a teacher in the school. It was pretty embarrassing. I'm totally convinced that the Lord saved my life by having me get caught the very first time I did it.

Ken Ruettgers
Author, Speaker
—And NFL Tackle

VITAL STATISTICS

Born August 20, 1962, in Bakersfield, California
6 feet 6, 292 pounds
College: University of Southern California
Position: Offensive Tackle
1996 team: Green Bay Packers

CAREER HIGHLIGHTS

- One of only nine Packers in team history who played on the team's offensive line for more than eleven seasons
- Selected Packers' 1987 Offensive Player of the Year, giving up just 3½ sacks all season
- Drafted in first round of NFL college draft (seventh player chosen)
- Named USC Offensive Player of the Year in 1984

WARMING UP

Ken Ruettgers, author, speaker, and veteran offensive tackle with the Packers, is no ordinary football player.

For instance, an average football player spends maybe five years in the league before injuries or a lessening of skills causes him to be cast aside and left with a career in insurance or annuities. Ken Ruettgers has been around the NFL for twelve years, long enough to put him in the company of Packer offensive linemen such as Jerry Kramer and Jim Ringo for longevity.

And an average football player may be one who plays the obligatory sixteen games and then hides for the next six months, unwilling to make a difference in the lives of real people. Ken Ruettgers doesn't run and hide when the uniforms are finally put away at Lambeau Field. He participates in such activities as the Packers' Speakers Bureau, the Packer 65 Sports Club (to benefit cystic fibrosis research), and helps with the Children's Miracle Network Telethon and the Diabetes Foundation.

Ken Ruettgers

Most of the time, Ken Ruettgers takes on the best sack specialist the Green Bay Packers' opponents can put on the field. Men like Neil Smith, Marco Coleman, Chris Doleman, and Fred Stokes.

But in 1995, Ruettgers took on a new opponent. A guy with a reputation for toughness, glib remarks, and a bit of braggadocio. A guy named Charles Barkley.

Yes, *that* Charles Barkley. The one with the strong inside moves, the sweet jumper, and the big mouth. The National Basketball Association Charles.

Ruettgers took on Charles in the arena of words. Challenged by Sir Charles's comments in a famous TV commercial, Ruettgers decided to set the record straight.

Perhaps you recall the commercial that turned Ken Ruettgers, football player, into Ken Ruettgers, author. It's not the one in which he pushes deodorant while talking about being civilized. It's not the one in which Larry Bird and Michael Jordan won't let him play HORSE.

It's the one in which Barkley boldly went where no athlete had gone before, declaring, "I am not a role model."

These words that launched a thousand columns in sports pages across the country also launched Ken Ruettgers on a crusade to correct what he thinks is a misunderstanding about athletes and role models. He interviewed fifty of his NFL colleagues and went through mounds of research, as well as thinking through his own ideas on the subject, in order to give readers a new appreciation for the importance of role models for today's children.

The result was *The Home Field Advantage*, a book far different from the kind usually churned out by athletes. No autobiography, although it has elements of Ruettgers's story mixed in, it is instead a call for adults, especially men, to take seriously their calling to be role models in life.

Some might find such a task to be an overly ambitious project for a football player. Yet Ken Ruettgers, author, speaker, and veteran offensive tackle with the Packers, is no ordinary football player.

For instance, an average football player spends maybe five years in the league before injuries or a lessening of skills causes him to be cast aside and left with a career in insurance or annuities. Ken Ruettgers has been around the NFL for twelve years, long enough to put him in the company of great Packer offensive linemen such as Jerry Kramer and Jim Ringo for longevity.

And an average football player may be one who plays the obligatory sixteen games and then hides for the next six months, unwilling to make a difference in the lives of real people. Ken Ruettgers doesn't run and hide when the uniforms are finally put away at Lambeau Field. He and his wife, Sheryl, have made their home in Green Bay, which enables him to take part in such activities as the Packers' Speakers Bureau, the Packer 65 Sports Club (to benefit cystic fibrosis research), and activities of a group called Pro Life Athletes. And when he is in his hometown of Bakersfield, California, Ruettgers hosts an annual golf tournament for the Boys and Girls Clubs, helps with the Children's Miracle Network Telethon and the Diabetes Foundation, and speaks in local schools.

An average football player may or may not have graduated from the college that paid his way through school to play football. Ruettgers not only graduated from USC with a degree in business administration, but later received an MBA from California State University, Bakersfield.

As a kid growing up in Bakersfield, Ken Ruettgers certainly didn't set out to become an author. He admits to being just a C student at Garces High School—hardly the stuff of young authors. Nor did he really set out to become a football player. It was his dad, Ron, who suggested he go out for the school team.

"I just want you to go out and try," the elder Ruettgers said. "Give it your best shot. Commit to it for one year. If you don't like it, you can always move on to something else."

"He was always good at not allowing us to quit what we had started," Ken says. "He made sure we saw it out."

Ken said yes, but that summer he burned his hand while trying to start a barbecue grill and couldn't play during the fall. But his dad persisted, and Ken went out for the team the following year. After four years of solid high school ball, Ruettgers pleased himself and his dad when he headed to the University of Southern California on a football scholarship.

It wasn't just talent or a persistent parent, though; Ken had done his part. When some of his high school coaches challenged him into serious, regular weight training, Ken agreed. "I had a good group of coaches. We had some coaches who were big into weightlifting. One of them had played some professional football."

His motivation increased as a high school sophomore after he noticed that some of his teammates were receiving letters from colleges. Ken asked one teammate, "Hey, why do you have that letter from Notre Dame?"

The player told his naive teammate, "If you play well enough in high school, they'll want you to play in college, and they'll pay for your college."

"You've got to be kidding me!" Ken responded. He had never before heard of such an intriguing prospect. It wasn't long until Ruettgers began to get those kinds of letters.

His school was small—about 450 students—but Ruettgers found that to be an advantage. "I could play both ways on the football team, and I could still run some track and play some basketball. It gave me an open door.

"I wasn't a real standout superstar guy," Ruettgers says, but he kept improving. And working hard. "I probably came on fairly strong my senior year. I was just a player who played well and was dedicated to working out and keeping my nose clean."

It was enough to bring on the scouts. All the Pacific-10 schools, as well as two Midwest giants, Michigan State and Notre Dame, wanted to talk with Ruettgers. Even a broken ankle late in his senior year didn't slow down the recruiting. Finally, Ruettgers signed with USC, eliminating the guesswork but bringing on a certain amount of fear.

"When I signed a letter of intent to go to USC, I remember all my friends saying, 'Oh, boy. He thinks he's going to USC! He'll never make it down there.' They had just been to the Rose Bowl, and Marcus Allen and Charles White were down there; so were Paul McDonald and Anthony Munoz. I had reservations myself. I had fear."

But Ken Ruettgers was ready. He had already survived much tougher circumstances than anything the SC offensive line could offer. When he was only eight years old, his mother had died from a brain tumor, leaving him, his two younger brothers, and his dad behind.

It was a difficult situation that was made bearable by the dedication of Ron Ruettgers, who would set the role model example that his sons would need. "My dad took care of us by himself for a couple of years, and that was big," Ruettgers says. "He completely committed his life to taking care of us. It's a lot of work to go to work and also take care of three kids."

But after two years of trying to go it alone, Ron Ruettgers remarried, which caused its own set of problems. "I really clashed heads with my step-mom," Ken says. "She came into a really difficult situation—an instant family of a husband and three kids, which would be difficult for anybody. She started setting some solid boundaries, which was good, but for a ten-year-old, all of a sudden all of these privileges that I thought I had were being taken away. It was very difficult for her to live up to the memories of my mother."

The passing of years and the gaining of spiritual maturity have helped to resolve those difficulties. "I have a great relationship with my dad, and a really neat relationship with my mom," Ken says.

The five years Ruettgers spent at USC (he sat out as a redshirt his freshman year because of injuries) were not typical years for the Trojans. Three of the five years, the team was on probation for various NCAA violations. Yet during his senior year, 1984, the team enjoyed its brightest moment in the California sun during his stay. In November, the Trojans defeated Number One Washington to earn their first trip to Pasadena in four seasons.

On this team of overachievers, the most famous of them all was perhaps linebacker Jack Del Rio, who was nominated for the Lombardi Award that year. At quarterback, the Trojans went with the forgettable Tim Green while Fred Crutcher was in charge of running the ball for the Trojan offense. In fact, the best part of the Trojan offense was the defense, which was remarkable, and which often gave the offense the ball in great field position.

So who among this collection of offensive players would take on the leadership role? The players began looking to Ruettgers, who was captain of the Trojans in this Rose Bowl season. And he performed, eventually being named as the team's Offensive Player of the Year. On a team with a tradition of great offensive threats like Marcus Allen and O. J. Simpson, it was an offensive lineman that year who captured the top award. "If you've got an offensive lineman making Offensive Player of the Year," Ruettgers says modestly, "that tells you that you don't have a lot of talent on offense."

But of course, USC has long had a fine reputation at that position as well. Some famous names have played on the Trojan line, dating all the way back to 1926, when a reserve tackle named Marion Morrison made the team. Of course, Morrison never made it in the NFL, but he did fine in Hollywood under the assumed name of John Wayne. Other linemen who made their marks include Keith Van Horne, (Chicago Bears), Jack Del Rio (Minnesota Vikings), and Hall of Famer Munoz (Cincinnati Bengals). Between 1968 and 1985, fourteen Trojan interior linemen were selected in the first round of the NFL draft.

Which is exactly where Ken Ruettgers would find himself on draft day 1985. He knew Philadelphia and San Diego wanted him and that Indianapolis and Atlanta had expressed interest. Sitting at his parents' home with several friends and Sheryl, "I was hoping for San Diego because it would keep me close to home.

"It was always a joke for the Southern Cal guys about going to a northern team. As a matter of fact, [teammate] Duane Bickett and I were coming out the same year, and we said, 'Anywhere but Buffalo and Green Bay.' . . . But then Green Bay picked me.

"I was surprised to go to Green Bay, but I was on cloud nine. The Packers traded up to snatch me." Ruettgers went in the first round, the seventh player selected in the draft.

But life is tough in the NFL, and Ruettgers wasn't sure he wanted to make a long-term career out of it. "I went in with my eyes kind of bugged open to do the best I could to fulfill expectations of a first-round pick, and I struggled. I remember I held out my first training camp, or a good chunk of it."

Despite the hold-out, Ruettgers established himself immediately as an important part of the Packer line. He played in all sixteen games that year and started two games. But the hard part wasn't over. "In the middle of my second training camp, I remember thinking, *Man, this is so difficult.* I just wanted to finish my four years [to qualify for the NFL pension plan] and move on to something else."

Author and football player Ruettgers hasn't retired yet, primarily for two reasons. The first would be to support his wife, Sheryl, and the second would be to honor his faith in Jesus Christ.

Ken and Sheryl Ruettgers first got together when he was in school at USC and dating her best friend. About a year and a half after that relationship soured, Ken and Sheryl began going out together.

"When I met Sheryl, I was going to church but she wasn't. So we started going to church together." Yet it wasn't until several years later—even after they were married—that the Ruettgerses trusted their lives to Jesus Christ.

"At different times in my life I felt committed to God," Ruettgers says about his spiritual journey. "Like when my mom died. But I think those were emotional commitments and not really from the heart. It wasn't until about 1992 that I really sold out for God.

"I think intellectually I had always known about Jesus, and if someone would have come up to me and asked the question Jesus asked Peter, 'Who do you say I am?' I could have answered correctly. But it wasn't until I got involved in an accountability group that I knew the Lord personally. My friends did a great modeling job and led me to Jesus. I gave up all that I was trying to hold on to. It just completely changed my life."

Since then, Ruettgers has become an outspoken person, using his platform as a pro football player to tackle various subjects close to his heart. One of those is the abortion issue.

In 1994, Ruettgers and former New York Giant offensive lineman Chris Godfrey got themselves into a bit of trouble because of their stance on that issue. A Wisconsin school had asked Ruettgers and Godrey to visit and speak about their view of abortion. Yet as the time for the meeting approached, the school was forced to cancel the visit because of the controversy it was stirring up in the town.

Later, a private school in the area invited them back. This time, there was no cancellation, but there was a large contingent of reporters there to cover their talk. Everything went well, but after the event a sports reporter published a scathing report about Ruettgers and his views on abortion. He implied that Ken and his football friends were better off to stay out of issues-oriented discussions and stick to the gridiron.

For weeks, the controversy went back and forth as supporters and detractors took sides and potshots on the subject. When the situation had died down and Ruettgers could reflect on it, he concluded that he had done the right thing. "Once you're convicted about what is right," he said, "don't let anyone stop you."

Whether in a classroom or on the field, Ken Ruettgers doesn't let much stop him. Throughout his long career in Green Bay, he has established himself as a dependable protector of the Packers' backfield. In a position where, as one player has said, "You know you're doing your job when you go unnoticed," Ruettgers has learned to take pride in his job.

And his job usually means taking on the key pass rusher from the other team. Although the negative statistics for an offensive lineman are usually the only ones he gets noticed for—offsides, holding, or other penalties—there have been times when Ruettgers has gotten attention for the positive part of his job.

Like in the season finale of his second year. The Packers were meeting the Super Bowl–bound New York Giants and their premier sack specialist, Lawrence Taylor. Taylor was on track to break the single season record for sacks in the season. All he needed was an average game against Ruettgers and the rest of the Packers' line. That afternoon, Ruettgers shut Taylor out, not allowing him to get to the quarterback even once.

And he also raised some eyebrows the next season when he allowed just 3½ sacks in the strike-shortened twelve-game season. For his efforts that season, Ruettgers enjoyed a little *déjà vu*. He was named the Packers' Offensive Player of the Year, just as he had been four years earlier as a senior standout with the USC Trojans.

Eight years later, the steady lineman had his most memorable season, as the 1995 Green Bay Packers came within one good quarter of getting to the Super Bowl. Riding the hot arm of Brett Favre, later named the league's most valuable player, and the strong play from the defense, the Pack won their division. They then manhandled the defending champion 49ers in the divisional playoff and gave the Dallas Cowboys about all they could handle in the conference championship.

Despite being author, speaker, and NFL tackle, Ruettgers is not one to look for glory. In fact, the verse he adds to his signature when he is asked for autographs is this: "He [Jesus] must become greater; I must become less."

"When I first read that, it stood out," Ken says. "Pro athletes struggle because people want to keep us on pedestals. Sports will do this. Just when you start believing the fans, someone else will come along to replace you. I put that on autographs to send the message."

When Green Bay Packer historians look back on the 1995 season, they'll surely mention Brett Favre's great year, the team's push for a Super Bowl berth, another interesting season for Reggie White, the success of Mike Holmgren, and the continued stability for a small-market team that is showing the big-market guys how to create fan loyalty and championship teams.

But they would do well to look also at the spiritual success of the Packers. It was a year that included a baptism in the team's Jacuzzi—a baptism that included Sheryl and Ken Ruettgers while chaplain Steve Newman and Rev. Reggie White officiated. It was a year that had many Packers meeting together in accountability groups, studying *The Seven Promises of a Promise-Keeper.*

"It was a highlight year from a professional standpoint," Ruettgers concludes. "But that really pales in comparison to what God has done in my life this year and how He has revealed Himself to me. It's been a unique situation on our team this year to see how God was moving."

Perhaps that can be the subject of another book by author and dominant NFL tackle Mr. Ruettgers.

Q & A WITH KEN RUETTGERS

Q: *What does the Ruettgers family like to do for recreation in the cold Green Bay winters?*
Ken: Everybody else in my family likes downhill skiing and cross-country skiing. Of course, with football, I can't do that until my playing days are over. We enjoy the snow and being out building snow people in it.

Q: *People sometimes wonder how athletes can give thanks after a win. What about the other team?*
Ken: I try to give thanks in all things, like the Bible says, which isn't always easy to do, especially after losing. But we must keep a biblical perspective. We should be thankful for all things. I try to thank God for whatever circumstances He puts me in.

Q: *What has been the greatest benefit of writing a book, with deadlines and all?*
Ken: [I think the book had value for me,] even if it had never been published. At one point in the process, I prayed, "Lord, I don't know what the purpose of this is, but if it is just to make known to me how important a model I am in my own family, and that starts with my relationship with You, then that will be a great blessing." And that has been the greatest blessing.

Q: *If a husband is to be the head of the home, how does he stop from dominating his wife?*
Ken: By serving her and by giving up our lives for our wives, as Christ did for the church. It's not always easy to do that, especially when we're blitzed with all kinds of other messages about wanting to fulfill our dreams and getting what we deserve. It's tough.

Q: *How do you and the Packers stay spiritually sharp?*
Ken: We have a couples' Bible study. We try to get couples who are engaged or just dating to come so we can do some modeling for them of what a Christian marriage looks like. We have a chapel service the day of the game. And the day after the game we have accountability groups of about four or five guys. It's a great blessing to see the Holy Spirit work on the guys' lives.

Junior Seau
Just Say Wow!

VITAL STATISTICS

Born January 19, 1969, in San Diego, California
6 feet 3, 255 pounds
College: University of Southern California
Position: Linebacker
1996 team: San Diego Chargers

CAREER HIGHLIGHTS

- Selected to Pro Bowl for five straight years (1991–1995)
- Named NFL Linebacker of the Year for two consecutive years (1993, 1994)
- 1994 NFL Man of the Year
- Played in one Super Bowl (1995)
- Voted NFL Defensive Player of the Year (1992)
- First-round draft pick in 1990 by the Chargers (fifth pick overall)
- College All-American (1989)

WARMING UP

Junior Seau is content to let his playing do the talking.

A case in point: The 1995 divisional championship game between the Pittsburgh Steelers and San Diego Chargers. The winner goes to Miami and the Super Bowl; the loser is relegated to six months of irritating questions from reporters. All week long, the Chargers had been looking for locker-room fodder—something the Steelers had said or done that they could use to motivate themselves.

The Chargers found plenty of it, from a mindless prediction by one Steeler that San Diego wouldn't score to the preparations the Steelers made before the game to record a Super Bowl rap video, perhaps like the Bears did in 1985. All the while the Chargers had kept relatively quiet, concentrating on their game plan.

When the game was over, it was the Chargers who had the bragging rights. By defeating the Steelers 17–13, San Diego earned a trip to the Super Bowl and suddenly discovered they could talk. Their quiet, professional determination to win turned to postgame celebration, as the Chargers basked in the newfound fame of Super Bowl ecstasy. Some of them yelled. Some of them trash-talked. Some of them reminded Pittsburgh about their ill-fated video.

But only Junior Seau remained quiet. To him, what he said on the field was enough.

Junior Seau

The back of his jersey says "Seau." His line of clothes gives the proper pronunciation, "Say Ow." But anybody who knows anything about the Chargers' number 55 is inclined to say, "Wow!"

Wow because Junior Seau curls 175-pound dumbbells, bench-presses 500 pounds, and squats 670 pounds.

Wow because at 6 feet 3 inches and 255 pounds, he can run the 40-yard dash in 4.61 seconds.

Wow because he has a vertical leap of 38 inches, putting him in the neighborhood of guys like Julius Erving—the grand poo-bah of all NBA dunkmeisters.

Wow because he has a home page on the Internet—not to tell everyone how good he is but mostly to let people know about the Junior Seau Foundation and to have a way to answer fan mail.

But *Wow* mostly because of the kind of person Junior Seau is.

Junior Seau has fashioned a football career out of making quarterbacks and running backs and anybody else who dares try to get past him say "Ow!" And with his blazing speed, catlike quickness, and brute strength, he has laid low more than his share of opposing players.

Yet if you were to ask Junior to say something about his football exploits, he would prefer to have you look up what he has done, lest he have to say anything about himself.

Both on and off the field, Seau is a man of action, not a man of words. Say what you want, that is a rarity in pro sports today.

Yes, Seau is content to let his playing do the talking. A case in point: The 1995 divisional championship game between the Pittsburgh Steelers and San Diego. The winner goes to Miami and the Super Bowl; the loser is relegated to six months of irritating questions from reporters. All week long, the Chargers had been looking for locker-room fodder—something the Steelers had said or done that they could use to motivate themselves.

The Chargers found plenty of it, from a mindless prediction by one Steeler that San Diego wouldn't score to the preparations the Steelers made before the game to record a Super Bowl rap video, perhaps like the Bears did in 1985. All the while the Chargers had kept relatively quiet, concentrating on their game plan.

When the game was over, it was the Chargers who had the bragging rights. By defeating the Steelers 17–13, San Diego earned a trip to the Super Bowl and suddenly discovered they could talk. Their quiet, professional determination to win turned to postgame celebration, as the Chargers basked in the newfound fame of Super Bowl ecstasy. Some of them yelled. Some of them trash-talked. Some of them reminded Pittsburgh about their ill-fated video.

But only Junior Seau remained quiet.

To him, what he said on the field was enough. And what he said on the Astroturf at Three Rivers Stadium could have been translated, "I want this game, if I have to win it single-handedly."

In fact, single-handed was how Seau was forced to play for most of the 1994–95 season. For most of the season, including the playoffs, Seau played with a pinched nerve in his neck. The injury was so bad that he had, as he says, "an arm I couldn't use and a shoulder that went numb every time I bumped into someone."

The injury would have put many lesser men on the shelf, but Seau played through the pain. He is convinced, though, that it was more than just Junior Seau wanting to play that got him on the field when everything in him told him not to play. And that's not even mentioning his wife, Gina, who, Seau admits, "wanted me to sit out and take care of it." In fact, although Gina preferred that her husband not play, she helped him in a vital way, simply because she knows what kind of man her husband is.

"Gina and I just prayed," Seau says. "I would come home and ice it down, and we would pray. I honestly believe that it had to be a power from above—from God—that helped me go through all that pain."

And there was the Seau desire to compete. "It was also the competitiveness in me. I felt that if I was doing something wrong where I'm not helping the team, then I would sit out, but until then, I was going to play."

Did he ever play against Pittsburgh! From the Steelers' first play from scrimmage, when Seau blasted to the left side of the line and wrapped up Barry Foster after a 2-yard gainer until their next-to-the-last play when Seau swallowed up Steeler running back John L. Williams, Seau was a defensive highlight film in the making.

Seau notched 16 tackles for his day's work and that coveted trip to Miami and a date with the San Francisco 49ers. And when it was all over and his teammates were celebrating their good fortune, the one-armed man sat quietly at his locker and talked about character. "You can never measure character, you can never measure heart," he said.

Another reason to say wow!

Junior Seau learned character at his daddy's knee. It was Tiania Seau who first began to teach his son the value of character. And he taught it to Tiania Seau Jr. and his six siblings in a number of ways.

The one that Junior remembers most was during the family's nightly Bible reading times. There in the Seau's two-bedroom house in Oceanside, California, the children knew exactly what was expected of them each night. They were to be in the house by five o'clock so they could be ready for family prayer at 5:30.

Promptly at that time, the family would sit down—Tiania Sr. and Luisa—surrounded by their brood. Then Dad Seau would read the Bible to the family in Samoan, their native language. "We had fifteen minutes of Scripture and then however long Dad wanted to take to close things out and have prayer," Junior recalls. "This is a time I will always be thankful for."

Growing up in the Seau family was a warm, spiritual experience, but it was not always easy. For instance, with nine members, the family was a bit too large for the house, so the four boys slept in the garage. It may not have been paradise, but they found something to like. "My sisters, who lived inside the house, always bragged that they had a carpet in their bedroom," Junior recalls. "But we'd say, 'So what? We have the biggest door in the whole place.'"

If you're going to live in a garage, you may as well take advantage of whatever freedom it offers, and the Seau boys certainly did that. They turned the garage-bedroom into a gym of sorts, using it to work out their intensely competitive natures.

They would use the garage as their site for numerous kinds of competitive activities as diverse as chess and weight-training. "We didn't have weights, but we made other things work." They would do push-ups and sit-ups by the hundreds, competing to see who could do the most sets. Then they would venture out behind the garage to a big maple tree, where they would do chin-ups. Or they would head down the street for a run.

The streets in Oceanside were often mean. The dangerous trifecta of drugs, gangs, and violence were hanging out at the corner, waiting to intercept good young men like the Seau brothers. Junior ran right past the trouble, in good measure because of the character his parents taught him.

"My drug was winning and competing," Seau says of those days in Oceanside. "I've always wanted to have my parents feel good. I wanted them to be proud of me, of what I'm doing, of what I am. I always did things that would make Mom and Dad happy. If I thought something was going to hurt Mom and Dad, I wouldn't do it. I still hurt when Mom and Dad are hurt. And that kept me out of a lot of trouble.

"They based what they taught me on the Bible. That is the rock and the base of our being. Without God and His Word, which He has left us, there isn't any answer. It gives you a sense of peace to know that Someone has been through this, and there are answers."

Most teenagers rebel a bit against their parents' values, their rules, and their standards, but Junior never succumbed to that temptation. "I can honestly say that what I received from Mom and Dad worked. Oh, I tested it a little, but I always came back to it."

When it came time to attend Oceanside High School, Seau entered with great expectations for what he could do in sports, especially in basketball, then "the love of my life," as Seau puts it.

And what he loved to do most was shoot. He describes himself as a "shooting forward. When I got the ball, the others just might as well back up for defense." He was good enough to be high school Player of the Year for all of San Diego after his senior season.

His basketball hero was Kareem Abdul-Jabbar, a man who Seau describes as someone who "played the game with class. He was an all-around man. He played the game the way it was supposed to be played."

Which is an apt description for how Junior himself plays another game—the one he has mastered at every level—football. As a senior he won another San Diego County Player of the Year award—two in fact— receiving both the offensive and defensive awards as an outstanding tight end and linebacker for the Oceanside Pirates. And, yes, he also was selected his area's Player of the Year in basketball. His football prowess, plus his 3.6 grade point average, earned him a trip up the road to the University of Southern California, where he expected to do great things on the gridiron.

That's when an unexpected, even unbelievable, thing happened to Seau. Although named to the California All-Academic Team with his 3.6 GPA, he failed to get passing grades on his college entrance exams. In spite of his strong grades in high school, he became a Proposition 48 player, which meant he was ineligible to play football during his freshman year at USC. He would have to get his grades up to a certain level, or he might never put on a football helmet again.

"That was hard for me," Seau says. "I was a three-sport guy and was always competitive. When they said 'Junior, you cannot play for a whole year,' it was like a little kid going to school, knowing that he wasn't going to get a treat at the end of the day.

"They took that treat away from me. I always went to school knowing that I was going to be able to play Friday on some kind of team. That had been my driving force, and I had to find a new driving force going into college, knowing that school was all I could compete in. It was humbling to know that I was going to have to struggle.

"To hear the Trojan band and hearing all the cheers that go up and the atmosphere of football and basketball and to know that I was not a part of it killed me."

It was the worst of times for Junior Seau.

Yet remember where he came from. Remember who his parents were. Remember what they taught him and who they taught him to trust. Junior had a disappointment on his hands, but he wasn't about to let it become a defeat.

"I knew, *It's up to me now.* I didn't have the pats on the back. I thought, *Who am I and what am I going to do with this obstacle in front of me?* No one else could have done anything for me."

He called the Proposition 48 situation "a blessing in disguise," a positive force. During his freshman year at USC he went to bed many nights disappointed, sometimes even crying in the college dorm, "knowing that Saturday's game was coming and I was not in it. I would hear the pep rallies going on." But, Junior adds, "It humbled me, and it helps me today.

"A lot of folks in the National Football League probably take football for granted. Well, I lost it for a year, and I know how it feels.

"My Prop. 48 year was a year in which I really drew close to God. I had no one else to rely on but Him. People like to associate with winners, and Junior was a loser. That's how people were perceiving me, and that's how I felt. I had to depend on prayer. I knew that I could depend on God and turn this around. But there was no guarantee. I had to make the grades."

He credits USC chaplain Tom Sirotnak with help along the way. Junior attended chapel services and listened to Sirotnak. There he also found an inner circle of Christian athletes he could belong to. "If I would have had football that first year at USC, I probably wouldn't hold on to Christ as much as I do today. It changed my life."

Of course, Seau made the grade and spent the next two seasons on the field as a key part of the USC Trojans team. In just two seasons for USC, Seau made his presence well known. As a junior, he was named All-American on the basis of his 19 sacks and 27 tackles behind the line of scrimmage. Then, in the Rose Bowl, he came up with a game-saving sack near the end to save the victory for USC over Michigan.

With a good junior year behind him and a promising NFL career ahead, Junior decided to forgo his last year of eligibility and enter the draft. One of his key considerations as he put his name up as one of several juniors in the draft—and one of five juniors who went in the top seven—was that he wanted to play for San Diego, just forty miles from hometown Oceanside. This was the first draft in which juniors were eligible to be signed by the NFL.

"Going into the draft, I had a good feeling that San Diego was going to draft me, but there was some interest from New England with the third pick. We had some conversations with San Diego prior to the draft, and we were just hoping and praying it would work out."

The Chargers' general manager, Bobby Beathard, had his heart set on Seau as much as Junior wanted to become a Charger. So when his name still appeared on the board at pick five, Beathard gobbled him up.

That was great news for Seau. In addition to wanting to play so close to home, he was decidedly against moving east.

"I didn't want to go to New England. It just didn't match. A guy with shorts and a tank top just wouldn't work in New England. There would be no market for my shorts," he says, laughing, referring to his "Say Ow" clothing line.

Back then, though, there were no "Say Ow" clothes, and there was just a young man from American Samoa by way of a tiny house in Oceanside. But that would all change with his high draft. It would be a time of adjustments.

And the first thing he would have to adjust to would be the fact that suddenly he was a rich young man. "I can't grasp a million dollars," he said soon after the draft. Some things in life are tougher to get used to than others. But for Seau, this newfound mountain of money has not seemed to be the barrier it is for so many of today's rich athletes. He has worked hard to turn his riches into opportunities for others.

"The greatest opportunity we have in the NFL is not that of personal fame, glory, or riches—it is to touch the lives of people and inspire them to achieve their dreams." Obviously Seau has made the adjustment to being a big-money player quite nicely.

Junior Seau has joined a growing number of Christian athletes who are using their wealth to help kids. Just as Darrell Green and Reggie White and others in football, and basketball's A. C. Green, David Robinson, and Kevin Johnson, have set up foundations to assist young people who need an extra boost in life, so has Seau.

In 1992, the Chargers star established the Junior Seau Foundation (JSF). "My hope is for this foundation to help kids face their life challenges with hope and dignity." To do that, the JSF tries to educate young people and give them a boost through child-abuse prevention efforts, drug and alcohol awareness, and anti-juvenile delinquency programs.

When Seau first signed with the Chargers he had a tough time grasping what it meant to be a millionaire. "When I came out in the draft, there was a lot of money slapped on me, and there were a lot of people coming after it." The foundation is one way he makes sure it goes to people who need it, especially promising teens.

One of JSF's biggest efforts is its Scholarship of Excellence. Each spring, JSF awards seventeen students with renewable $1,000 college scholarships.

"What I try to do with the kids and the foundation is to give them some of the experiences I've gone through and I hope they can take what they need. I want them to know that things don't just happen. I'm a part of this elite group in the NFL because of a lot of work. I tell them that they're going to go through a lot of trials and obstacles, but they have to overcome them."

The National Football League has recognized Seau's contributions to the young people of San Diego by naming him the 1994 True Value NFL Man of the Year. Of his efforts, Seau says simply, "I feel fortunate to have the opportunity to use my platform in the NFL to help kids. I'm not a player who's going out there and just playing for the glory and the money. If I can [help] the youth of San Diego, then I've accomplished something special."

The list of men who have captured the NFL's Man of the Year Award includes a number of players, who, like Seau, are Christians. Included in that elite group are Anthony Munoz (1991), Mike Singletary (1990), Steve Largent (1988), Reggie Williams (1986), Rolf Benirschke (1983), and Roger Staubach (1978). It's a distinguished group of caring football players.

Standing beside Seau in both his on-the-field and off-the-field activities is Gina, whom he married in 1991. The two met at the NFL Fastest Man Competition in 1990 when they "bumped into each other," as he puts it. There were no injuries, for he elaborates, "she was working, and I was walking by, we saw each other, and that was it."

Well, there was a courtship and all that, but the two seemed to be attracted to each other immediately. It made things easier that Gina DeBoer worked for the Chargers at the time. "When I went to the Chargers training camp, she was there again. She's also a Christian, and we had the same type of traits." After March 14, 1991, they had the same last name too.

Between then and now, Gina Seau's husband has exploded onto the NFL scene as one of its greatest players ever. In the first season after they were married, 1991, Junior rose to the top of his game. He became the Chargers' top defensive playmaker, with 129 tackles and 7 sacks. Against their NFC rival Los Angeles Rams, he made 13 tackles, 11 of them solos. He was named to his first Pro Bowl and was developing his characteristic style of lining up at both inside and outside linebacker positions—or anywhere along the defensive line. He began to play football intensely, as only a few others have, using his one-line defensive motto: "If there's a football on the field, I'm going after it."

As the years wore on and Seau began to pick up every award possible for a defensive player, his game continued to improve. Perhaps former Cleveland Browns coach Bill Belichick put it best when he said, "Junior Seau is the best defensive player we've faced, I'd say by a pretty good margin. He does it all. He can play at the point of the attack, he chases down plays, he plays the run, he plays the pass. He's a guy nobody's really been able to stop."

And finally, in 1994, he was playing for a team that was hard to stop. Not that anyone predicted it for the Chargers that year and many sportswriters picked the club to hang around the bottom of the division once again. The Chargers had made the playoffs in only one of the previous eleven seasons. Picked by many to hang around the bottom of the division, it looked like more of the same at Jack Murphy Stadium. Many doubted whether their quarterback, Stan Humphries, could do anything to change the chargers direction.

All the Chargers did, to the surprise of every NFL watcher north and east of San Diego, was to win their first six games on their way to an 11–5 finish and first place in the AFC West. Then, in a game with a heart-stopping finish, the Chargers edged Miami 22–21 for the right to face Pittsburgh in that game in which Junior Seau showed the world how to play inside linebacker.

Two weeks after the Pittsburgh game, San Diego fell in the Super Bowl to the San Francisco 49ers, 49–26. In what has become a typical outing for Seau, he recorded 11 tackles and 1 sack as he did all he could to avoid another loss for the American Football Conference.

How does a man like Junior Seau respond to the sadness of losing the biggest game of his life? And would he even be offended to have such a question asked? Some are, of course. And some players can treat questions that hit too close to home as coming from mortal enemies. But to even suggest that Junior Seau would respond in any way but as a gentleman would do him a disservice.

"I don't judge people on what they say and how they say things," Seau responds when asked about being asked about Super Bowl XXIX.

"We played a game that they want to talk about, that's how I look at it. Whether it's good or bad, you have to report it. And that's how I deal with it. Losing the Super Bowl isn't the end of the world. We are still healthy. We are able to go back and correct our mistakes and give it another try. That's the positive side. The negative side is that we didn't perform the way we wanted to and we got beat. It's as simple as that."

Say Wow!

It's not often that a man like Junior Seau comes along. Thoughtful in his treatment of others and dedicated to making himself a better player. Caring in a sincere way, without any showboating, for the needs of those less fortunate than himself. Devoted in his trust of God. Respectful in his words and actions.

On the back of the winter 1995 edition of an NFL publication called the *NFL Report* is an advertisement imploring young people to "Get Out And Play Football." Hovering over the copy and pictures of children playing football is, appropriately enough, Junior Seau. Near him is a caption that reads, "Pretend you're Junior Seau—he's Bionic."

Nah, he's not bionic. He may have muscles of steel, but he's for real. He may be able to hunt down a ball carrier like he has radar, but he's all natural. He may seem to play through pain as if he's made of ropes and pulleys, but he hurts like the next person.

He's just a kid from Southern California who learned to speak English after he was seven years old and learned to trust Jesus Christ at about the same time.

He's got a wife with whom he reads the Bible and prays every day. He's got two little children named Sydney Beau and J. R. whom he takes with him to church—where he is as active as he can be. And he's got a whole city full of kids in San Diego that he wants to help.

He's a guy who, with Gina, tries "to be the best Christians and the best people we can be. What we want to do is treat everyone fairly and be good people."

Bionic? No. Special? Yes.

Say Ow?

Say Wow!

Q & A WITH JUNIOR SEAU

Q: *What is the worst thing about being an NFL star?*
Junior: You definitely lose your privacy. And that is hard. The only privacy you have is at home, and sometimes the phone goes crazy and you can't deal with that either.

Q: *What keeps you going when things get tough?*
Junior: If I didn't have my priorities straight, I don't think I would have been able to survive as long as I have. My faith works all the way around. Any decision that my wife and I have, we pray about it.

And as odd as it may sound to some people, it works for us. We're proud of it.

Q: *What drove you to play so well in the 1995 playoff game against Pittsburgh?*
Junior: We were close to our goal. I had always dreamt of going to the Super Bowl. I had always wanted to help my hometown get to the Super Bowl.

You know, I can't even remember half of the game. I've never watched a replay of it. Yet, it was a victory that I'm always going to remember. It's something that my wife and I look back on and know that we are really blessed to go out there and do what we did.

Reggie White
No Introduction Needed

VITAL STATISTICS

Born December 19, 1961, in Chattanooga, Tennessee
6 feet 5, 300 pounds
College: University of Tennessee
Position: Defensive End
1996 team: Green Bay Packers

CAREER HIGHLIGHTS

- NFL's all-time sack leader
- Chosen NFL Defensive Player of the Year (1991, *Pro Football Weekly*)
- Named Defensive Lineman of the Year (1990)
- Named Defensive Lineman of the Year (1990)
- Selected NFL Player of the Year (1988, Washington Touchdown Club)
- Selected NFL Defensive Player of the Year (1987)
- Named Most Valuable Player of 1986 Pro Bowl
- Named NFC 1985 Rookie of the Year
- Chosen College All-American (1983)

WARMING UP

While in his second season with Memphis, Reggie White asked his agent to get him to the NFL. By September, he was a Philadelphia Eagle. He had already played an entire season in the USFL, and now he was suiting up to do the same in the NFL. By the end of 1985 Football Season II, White had racked up 13 sacks and the NFC Defensive Rookie of the Year Award.

At this point in his career, Reggie White was still someone who needed an introduction. Sure, he had received some awards in college and had played well for the Eagles in his first year, but he was just one of dozens of good defensive ends in the league.

As his career picked up steam, though, and as reporters talked with him, White eventually came to be regarded as one of the best interviews in the league. Yet he never backed down from talking about his faith.

Reggie White

I n the crowded field of football players called the National Football League, it is not easy for a player to achieve a high degree of name recognition.

After all, there are about 1,600 players in the NFL, and there aren't many fans who can keep them all straight. And frankly, there are only so many high-profile position players—quarterbacks and running backs—who attract most of the ink, air time, and fame.

That's why it's a bit unusual that one of the household names in the NFL belongs to Reggie White, a defensive end. Yet for most fans, Reggie White needs no introduction. He has established himself to such a degree that his name is breathed in the same excited tones as those of Steve Young, Troy Aikman, and Barry Sanders.

Yet, because of his entry via the United States Football League (USFL) and his unusual pursuits, many fans have forgotten more about Reggie White than they know about most other players.

Perhaps a bit of a refresher about Reggie would be in order, especially since his pro career has now spanned twelve seasons. Did you know the following?

- Reggie White's first two years of his pro career were spent with the Memphis Showboats of the USFL.
- During that second year as a pro (1985), Reggie played in thirty-five games. He suited up for the entire USFL season and then moved on to Philadelphia for the NFL season.

- Reggie White became known as the Minister of Defense while he was still in college.
- Reggie White does very good impersonations of famous people, including Muhammad Ali, Rodney Dangerfield, Elvis, and Bill Cosby (as a comedian, not as a football player for hapless Temple).
- Reggie wants to build a religious theme park in Tennessee.
- Reggie White loves big-time wrestling.

Seems like the answer to a football trivia question—you know, "Who played in thirty-five pro football games one season and does a great impersonation of Bill Cosby?" It points to the diversity of this man whom everyone seems to know yet remains a mystery to a lot of people. What is it that shaped him into an incredible athlete with a burning desire to keep getting better, that gave him a genuine love for people and a fire in his heart for issues like race relations, his faith, and family?

For all of us, what makes us into who we become is a combination of factors, and we may never know exactly which factors are most important. But for Reggie White, the key factors are a mother, a grandmother, a couple of pastors, and a coach—all people who influenced his life while he was growing up in Chattanooga, Tennessee, in the '60s and '70s.

"My mother is a strong person," Reggie says. "I thank God for her." His mom was a single parent, but she was not truly alone in her task of raising Reggie and his older brother. There was also his grandmother and the occasional help from his father.

But at the beginning, it was Mom who set the tone for a kid growing up in an all-black area of Chattanooga. "She used positive and negative discipline," he recalls, stressing that "negative discipline" is not the same as physical abuse. "My mother, when it was time for something to be done, she wanted it done. She was the one who gave out the discipline."

There came a point, though, in young Reggie's life when Thelma Collier left the home. She married Reggie's stepdad, who was in the service, and decided to follow him and his travels. Reggie, who had no desire to travel, asked to stay with his grandmother. For the next two years, Grandma took care of him.

And she took him to church. It was an all-black church with a white preacher named Reverend Ferguson, and it was through this pastor that White came to a saving knowledge of Jesus Christ. "When I was thirteen years old, I accepted Christ as my Savior," he recalls. "It was Reverend Ferguson's care for the church and for the children of the church that really made an impact on me. It was the kind of life I wanted to live."

Later, when White was eighteen, another pastor, Jerry Oakes, provided another level of spiritual help. "I think the greatest influence for me spiritually was Pastor Oakes," White says. "He was the one guy during my lifetime who I could always call on when I had serious problems: people hurting me, things I did to people, handling temptation. He helped me through those times."

And White also received a great amount of help from a high school basketball coach at Howard High School, Robert Perden. "He saw something in me I didn't see in myself," Reggie explains. "He told me as a junior in high school that I had the potential to be the best defensive lineman in pro football."

Young Reggie White did not listen to Coach Perden solely because he had such high praise for Reggie. "I listened to him because I respected him as a person. He cared for me; I cared about him."

In reality, the two had a bit of a strange relationship—not one you would hear recommended at a coaches' clinic. The two of them would often wrestle, and the coach would win. He would manhandle White so much that the high schooler would cry. Then one day during basketball practice, the coach hit Reggie in the chest. White began to cry, which just made the coach get into his face even more. "Until you come back and make sure you're tough, I'm going to keep doing it," he told the teary hoopster.

It took a couple of years for Reggie to figure out and appreciate what the coach was doing. "He tried to build some toughness in me. That helped me in my career."

And it helped White's own self-esteem that he defeated the coach the last time they wrestled.

But it was more than with basketball that Coach Perden helped White. "He talked to me about God, about life in general. If I had problems, I knew I could go to him when I couldn't go to anybody else."

So throughout his formative years, Reggie White had a group of people who instructed him, challenged him, and disciplined him.

Their help guided him through incidents of discrimination, like the time when he was eleven and was walking with a white girl through his neighborhood. A white motorist pulled along beside him and yelled at him to leave the girl alone.

Their counsel helped him when he was in college at the University of Tennessee, struggling with the difficult temptation of women. "That was real hard to overcome," he says.

And the direction of his coach helped him as he developed into one of the best college football players in the country. Dale Haupt, who was the Philadelphia Eagles' defensive line coach when White played for Philly, recalls seeing him at Tennessee. "What you really noticed was his strength and explosion. He was bull-rushing his guy backward."

This is not the way Reggie White began his career at Tennessee. In fact, when he first started down the college football road, he was anything but an attacking, blitzing, flailing football player who would go through any wall to make the play.

Not that he was a slouch. He was good enough through his sophomore year to be projected as a possible All-American as a junior. However, he didn't have a very good work ethic.

"When I was ready to work out, I would ask the other guys if they wanted to join me. If they didn't, then I wouldn't either. I pretty much based my work ethic on what others would do."

On the field, things went from hopeful to hopeless. "I went to pre-camp and hurt my ankle. I played in the first game, which I shouldn't have. Then I missed the second game. My ankle got well, and then I hurt my other ankle. Then I chipped a bone in my heel. I had a terrible season.

"The reason this happened was because I didn't take a leadership role. I chose to be a follower, instead of a leader. I depended on other people, instead of depending on God."

White learned his lesson. "The next year, I worked as hard as anybody, depending on nobody to go around with me. When I started running, when I started lifting, everybody else started doing the same thing, and that year our defense went from 99th in the country to 9th.

When his career at Tennessee was over, White faced a big decision. Would he take the normal path to stardom and head for the NFL, or would he take a chance on the new, upstart United States Football League? The USFL played its games in the spring and early summer, culminating in a championship game in August.

Either way, White would be a high pick, for many were calling him the best defensive lineman available in the draft. In the end, the decision was strongly influenced by his girlfriend's being a student at East Tennessee; Reggie wanted to be close to her. So he signed with Memphis in the USFL. Of course, it didn't hurt that the Showboats offered him a five-year, $4 million contract.

Throughout his time with Memphis, White continued to use his newfound work ethic for the team's good. "When I went to the USFL, my work habits were the same. I promised myself there would never be an off-season, that I would commit myself to prepare for the season. From that point on, I've tried to figure out things that I need to do to get better."

In his second USFL season, White began to worry about the league's instability, and he discovered that he wanted to prove himself against the more established NFL competition. While in his second season with Memphis, White asked his agent to get him to the NFL. By September, he was a Philadelphia Eagle. He had already played an entire season in the USFL, and now he was suiting up to do the same in the NFL.

With that extra season under his belt, he went to work in his first NFL game, recording 10 tackles and being credited with 2½ sacks. By the end of the 1985 Football Season II, White had racked up 13 sacks and the NFC Defensive Rookie of the Year Award.

At this point in his career, Reggie White was still someone who needed an introduction. Sure, he had received some awards in college and had played well for the Eagles in his first year, but he was just one of dozens of good defensive ends in the league.

While in his third year in the league, Reggie and the Eagles played Chicago. It was a big game because it represented the return of Philadelphia coach Buddy Ryan to Soldier Field, where he had directed the Bears defense into a revitalized Monster of the Midway that helped Chicago win Super Bowl XX. After the Bears-Eagles game, the locker room was crawling with reporters, and some of them ended up at Reggie's locker. They began to ask him some questions, and he dutifully began to answer. But the reporters quickly began to click off their recorders and slink away, for Reggie White was talking to them about faith in God, and they didn't know how else to respond. "I guess I scared you off," Reggie told the reporters as they departed.

As his career picked up steam, though, White eventually came to be regarded as one of the best interviews in the league. Yet he never backed down from talking about his faith. In fact, it became the expected answer from him. He had been dubbed the Minister of Defense while in college, and reporters finally caught on that he was serious about it.

White's climb to fame may have begun in earnest early in 1987 at the Pro Bowl. Selected to his first postseason all-star game, he made the most of it, recording 4 sacks and being named the game's most valuable player. Add to that during the season he finished second only to Lawrence Taylor in sacks (20½ to 18), and you've got the makings of a star in the NFL. Slowly, Reggie White was coming into his own.

Each year in Philadelphia gave White new reasons to shine. In 1987 he led the league in sacks with 21, despite playing in only twelve games because of the strike. In 1988, he again led the NFL in sacks, but this time he was given an extra bonus. He was named the NFL Player of the Year. No longer would reporters walk away from a Reggie White comment.

But the time would come for White to walk away from the team he had played for since 1985. In 1993, the NFL was ready to institute free agency into its system of player relations. For Reggie White, it was possibly time to move on. As the real season wound down and the signing season began, White began to indicate that he had doubts about the Eagles' commitment to fielding a championship team.

The Eagles had a February 28 deadline. Until then, they alone could negotiate with White. But after that, he would be an unrestricted free agent, able to sign with anybody. First, though, he had to deal with Philadelphia. In early February, he met with the mayor of the City of Brotherly Love, Ed Rendell. The mayor used the "local sports heroes need to stay loyal" theme in his discussions with White.

Then the folks of Philly did their best to persuade White to stay. In an early March rally, 3,500 Eagles fans turned out at downtown JFK Plaza to noisily ask White to stay. Big number 92 sent a message to the assembled throng, telling them, "I certainly have not closed the door on returning to Philadelphia." Yet White was still expressing concern that the Eagles' brass had not made a "commitment to win."

By the next weekend, White was off on what can best be described as a bizarre dog-and-pony show, during which he was ushered from city to city by NFL owners who wanted him to work for them.

No fewer than nine teams wooed White. It finally came down to San Francisco, Washington, and Green Bay. The Packers seemed unlikely, for the Packers represented the smallest market in the NFL, hardly the place for a rich millionaire who wanted to pour his heart and money into the inner city. Besides, the rich Packer tradition of Super Bowl appearances was more than two decades past. This seemed to mitigate against White's other concern—playing for a championship.

Throughout White's search for a new football home, one overriding factor controlled his move. He wanted to do what God wanted him to do. "I was afraid I would make the wrong decision," he would say later. "San Francisco and Washington—those situations probably looked better than anybody's because their teams were probably going to continue to win.

"I came out and said I wanted to go to a team that I felt was going to win. I wanted to win a championship immediately, and those two teams probably provided that opportunity faster than some of the other teams.

"But I couldn't make a decision on that basis. I had to be able to make a decision on where God wanted me to be. I never thought He would want me to be in Green Bay.

"Then a Christian brother shared with me that God told him to tell me not to worry about the [inner-city] ministry, that He would take care of the ministry."

One factor that may have played into the mix is that Mike Holmgren, the head coach of the Packers, is a fellow Christian. One person close to Holmgren reported that when Reggie saw a report about Holmgren's faith in *Sports Spectrum* magazine, he was in the final stages of making his decision.

"When I came down to the decision," White says, "it didn't shout at me. God gave me the opportunity to be with a team that I think is going to win. It has good young players, it has a commitment to win, and it has good coaches I'm excited about."

The decision to go to Green Bay, of course, did not please everyone. This much-publicized Reggie-watch left many people puzzled, and it left many critical of White.

"Most critics said that I went after the money," says White. "I said that I would let God make the decision, and a lot of people made jokes about it. But I praise God, because it gave me an opportunity to be persecuted, and the Bible says we should rejoice in persecution. I know what God is doing in my life, and I know that God has entrusted to me the situation I have."

It's been a few years now since Reggie made that decision to go to Green Bay. How has it panned out for the Minister of Defense?

From a football standpoint, it enabled him to get to the very doorstep of the Super Bowl in 1996 when the Packers played the Cowboys in the NFC championship game. Although the Pack lost and prolonged Reggie's lifetime search for a spot in the Super Bowl sun, the incidents that led up to the game gave him ample new opportunities to witness of the power of God.

During the final weeks of the 1995 NFL season White suffered first an injury and then a fire at his church. Both incidents could have devastated a player. But White's faith and perseverance sustained him to turn these apparent losses into gains.

On December 3, in a game against the Cincinnati Bengals, White strained his left hamstring. At first, it seemed to be an inconsequential injury, especially since Reggie White was not one to miss a game because of a strained muscle. After all, he had played in 175 straight games.

By the next game, though, Reggie had not recovered. For the first time in his career, he stood helplessly on the sideline as his teammates lost to the Tampa Bay Bucs in overtime. His hamstring was not responding.

Four days later, even worse news was coming out of Green Bay. Reggie had met with his teammates to tell them that his season was over. He would have to have surgery on his hamstring, and he would not be back. The Packers, who knew they had a team that could challenge for the NFC title behind Brett Favre, now had to resign themselves to facing the rest of the season and the playoffs without the anchor of their defense.

"We're all shocked," said tight end Mark Chmura. "We lost one of our leaders."

Dr. Patrick J. McKinzie, the team's doctor, was lined up to do the surgery. For his part, White said, "I'm not blaming anybody. I am not blaming God. It is just a situation that happened."

But what happened next was remarkable.

That night, Reggie went home to his family. As he was playing with his children, Jeremy and Jecolia, he noticed that as he ran his hamstring felt better than it did the day earlier.

In a flash, he was on the phone with strength and conditioning coach Kent Johnston, and soon the two were at Lambeau Field, testing the leg. Finding it to be in amazingly good shape, they hopped in the car and drove over to Mike Holmgren's house.

"I was turning out the Christmas lights, and he was there," says Holmgren. "I thought it was Santa."

Santa couldn't have done better himself.

The next day, White ran through a series of tests, and was found fit to play on Sunday. The surgery was canceled.

"It's another situation where something miraculous happened," White explained that day. "I thank God for it. I can't explain it. I can't explain why my leg's not hurting as bad as it was Tuesday."

White was able to play the rest of the season, leading the Pack into the playoffs and the championship game against the Cowboys.

And then there was the fire.

Just days before that big game with Dallas, the country was shocked by the news that White's home church in Knoxville, Tennessee, where he spends his off-season, had burned. When officials of the predominantly African-American church stopped by the church to pick up some papers in the aftermath of the fire, they found racial slurs spray-painted on the walls.

White, an associate pastor of the church, reacted with understandable pain. "I'm upset because it's a lot more than a church being burned down," he said.

Yet he saw hope amid the tragedy. "I would hope that people of all races would rally together and begin to fight against this."

Sadly, the incident also dredged up for Reggie the recollection of an earlier tragedy in his family. Four years earlier, his stepfather had been murdered in Chattanooga, and the killer had never been found.

White feared that the same thing would happen in Knoxville; that another crime would go unpunished.

After that difficult week, White spent the closing minutes of the championship game on the Eagles bench, watching the Cowboys win another NFC title. And for once, White lost his cool. As he sat dejectedly on the bench after the game, cameras were thrust near him as the crew sought to record his sorrow. Uncharacteristically, White stood and demanded that the crew get the cameras away from him.

Much was made of White's postgame actions, but he's not one to back down from what he has done. Just as he was upset by the week's proceedings when the great injustice was done at his church, so he had feelings for the bitter loss to the Cowboys.

Reggie White does not profess to be perfect. He only professes to have a genuine love for Jesus Christ and a desire to serve Him with his life. One who, despite his faults, wants to be a role model for those who observe him.

"We talk about role models, but the Bible says in the book of Psalms, let the godly man be your hero. I would say that Reggie White is doing all he can to live the life God has called him to live, so if you look at Reggie White as your role model, make him your role model because he's a man of God, not because he plays football, not because of his stats. The question is, when we die, did our life have an impact, and will it continue to have an impact? I'm not perfect, but I'm striving for perfection. I want to be like God."

But before White reaches out to a community or to the country as a role model, he is careful to make sure he is the kind of person at home he needs to be.

"My responsibility to my kids is to be their father, and be my wife's husband. If I'm not being the father and husband I need to be, how can I be a role model to other people's kids? A lot of us put on a facade; you act one way outside the house, and another way at home. I don't want to be that way. I don't want to be a phony.

"I don't want my wife looking at me funny when I'm trying to do good. I don't want my kids looking at me and saying, 'Yeah, he's trying to be good for everybody else, but he can't be good to us.' I've got to make sure not to be good just to other people; I've got to be good at home. When I get it right at home, it's easy to be good and right to other people, because my kids can say to those other people, 'This is the way my dad is at home.' And my wife can say, 'That's the way my husband is at home.'"

Consistency. That's what his family sees; that's what a generation of football fans see. Reggie White has become a household word that is synonymous with winning, class, dedication, love of God, and love of family. He's the kind of man we need to be introduced to more often in the world of sports.

Q & A WITH REGGIE WHITE

Q: *How do you deal with living under the microscope of being in the NFL?*
Reggie: It is tough. But it is a requirement for growth. And I have to grow if I'm going to have an impact on people. I have to gain a closer relationship with the Lord. I've learned that it really isn't what I say that's important, but it's how I live.

Q: *Do you feel any conflict in playing a game that could be considered violent while preaching about Jesus?*
Reggie: Football is aggressive, but it is not violent. Violence is what's happening on our streets. I get upset when the game is labeled violent, because it isn't. We're not killing each other. We don't go out with the idea of ending someone's career.

Q: *You have a big interest in helping those in the inner city. What is the state of things within the cities?*
Reggie: The church has to come to a point where we are the ones to help provide the needs of the people instead of making the people depend on government. The government should be responsible, because we're paying our taxes. But the government isn't going to take the responsibility that the church should, because the answer is Jesus Christ. When He healed people, when He fed people, He met their needs.

Right now, I don't think the majority of the unsaved people in our country see hope in the church. We've got to allow people to see hope in the church. We've got to show them that God is good.

Q: *What drives you to make the extra effort?*
Reggie: The better shape I'm in, the more confident I am. It gives me the opportunity to do the things God's called me to do.

I was watching TV and saw some kids in Brazil, the street kids. Businessmen had hired policemen to kill these kids, because they wanted to get them off their businesses, and these kids were getting slaughtered.

I have an opportunity. God has given me this game as a platform to proclaim the name of Jesus. I think when I see that kind of thing and go out in some of these neighborhoods, it drives me even more to want to be great because I think greatness in my profession gives me the opportunity to get in doors normally people can't get in. That drives me more and more. Every time I want to quit, I just start thinking of people who are locked out of opportunities.

Q: *What role has your wife played in your life?*
Reggie: Sara has helped me so much in my life. . . . She's brought out of me things I didn't know were in me. She has helped my character. God put the right woman in my life.

Q: *What advice do you have for kids who sometimes hang out with the wrong people?*
Reggie: There's a Scripture verse that says, "Foul company corrupts good morals," and if we continue to hang around bad company, I don't care how righteous we may be, we're going to be corrupted in some way. Good company will help uplift our morals and continue to show us what's right and what's wrong.

PART TWO

THE YOUNG WARRIORS

Trev Alberts
Never on a Sunday?

VITAL STATISTICS

Born August 8, 1970, in Cedar Falls, Iowa
6 feet 4, 245 pounds
College: University of Nebraska
Position: Linebacker
1996 team: Indianapolis Colts

CAREER HIGHLIGHTS

- Made 8 tackles and deflected one pass during first pro start
- First-round draft pick in 1994 by the Colts (fifth pick overall)
- Received 1993 Butkus Award as outstanding college linebacker
- Named college All-American (1993)

WARMING UP

Since the Alberts family loved Iowa football, it seemed to be a no-brainer that when Trev turned out to be an outstanding high school football player, he would turn to Iowa City for his college career. In fact, only the University of Iowa and Iowa State actively recruited him. So, true to what everyone expected, Trev made an oral commitment to attend Iowa and spend the next four or five years as a Hawkeye.

But then, in a surprise move, he got a feeler from out of state.

"I got a call from Nebraska, and the coaching staff asked me for a recruiting visit," Alberts recalls. "Actually, they offered me a scholarship before I even went. So, even though I had committed orally to Iowa, I decided, 'Let's just go out there and see what they have.'"

What they have in Lincoln, Nebraska, is Coach Tom Osborne, a man who is noted for his Christian faith and for his concern and care for his players. And, oh, yes, he also has a rather remarkable record as a football coach. At that point he hadn't led Nebraska to a national collegiate championship, but everyone knew it was just a matter of time till it would happen.

"I was able to sit down with my mom and dad and listen to Coach Osborne talk. We asked him about his faith. He said stuff like, 'We don't practice on Sunday. That's the Lord's Day.' Things like that I didn't find anywhere else in college football."

Trev Alberts

Each Sunday during the pro football season Trev Alberts roams the defensive line for the Indianapolis Colts, seeking out the quarterback to wreak havoc on the guy before he gets rid of the ball. Just as he did as an All-American linebacker at Nebraska, Alberts sometimes manhandles opponents and appears to relish what he is doing.

To tell the truth, though, Alberts isn't very happy about it.

Don't get the wrong idea. The football part he loves. Plus, he was born to play linebacker, so it's not the position that's a problem. And he's plenty happy playing for the Indianapolis Colts. After all, they're paying him several million dollars to rush quarterbacks and swallow up runners.

It's the Sunday part of the equation that bothers him.

If Trev Alberts were king of the world, the National Football League would play its sixteen games on a different day. Never on Sunday.

To understand why, we have to go to Iowa, where Alberts grew up. Cedar Falls, to be exact. And we have to go back to the time before football became such a big deal around the Alberts home. Back to a time when football was really no deal at all.

In the Alberts home, which consisted of Mom, Dad, Trev, his older brother Troy, and his little sister Tammy, life could be summed up with three words: family, farming, and faith.

The family lived in the 30,000-inhabitant city of Cedar Falls, but they farmed a 300-acre section of Iowa that lay about thirty-five miles outside town. It was a family farm that was passed down from Trev's paternal grandpa when he died of cancer at age fifty-five. Trev's mom and dad, who met in college, didn't want to live on a farm; indeed, Mrs. A had told Mr. A early in their marriage that she had no interest in being a farmer's wife.

So after buying the farm, the family stayed in the city and commuted to the farm on Saturdays and evenings to work the corn and soybean fields. All the while, Dad Alberts kept his day job. This meant that his two strapping boys, Troy and Trev, had to be available to help.

That, in part, explains why football didn't make much of an inroad into the Alberts household. Oh, they would cheer for the hallowed Iowa Hawkeye football team, as any good Iowa family does, but the family was simply too busy for the boys to pursue football in a personal way.

But it wasn't all work for this family. There was also time for church. Sunday mornings meant no farming and no work, only time in "the Lord's house" to worship.

"I attended church ever since I was a baby," Alberts recalls. "My parents made a real commitment that regardless of how much work had to be done on the farm, it never came before Wednesday night prayer meeting or Sunday services. We were always at Cedar Falls Gospel Hall."

During some periods, that "always" was frequent. "I remember that we would have times when we would have preachers come for six weeks at a time. Every night for six weeks, they'd preach the gospel."

What Trev learned at all those meetings paid off when he was just eight years old, for that was when he accepted Jesus Christ as his Savior.

At age six, Trev remembers, "I knew that if I died as I was, I knew where I was going to go." That year a guest preacher, Bill Lavery, visited the church one Sunday, and gave an evening sermon that Trev calls "kind of a hellfire-and-brimstone message."

"I knew right then that I was scared to death of ever going through that. But the feeling kind of passed. I'd be all concerned about it, but everything else would kind of get in the way. The devil would come in and try to take some of those thoughts out of my mind. And I think too that my parents felt, 'He's awfully young.'

"When I was eight years old, my dad was on a business trip to California, and I asked my mom to get me out some tracts or something. I wanted to get this thing settled. She went through verse after verse after verse, and one of the first verses she read to me was John 6:47, 'Verily,

verily, I say unto you, He that believeth in Me hath everlasting life'"
(KJV). Mom continued to go on, but Trev was confused. "I got to the
point where I said, 'I'm just going to go to hell. I don't get this.'

"It wasn't long after that when I finally got it. I realized there was
nothing for me to do. The Bible doesn't say I have to pay God a million
dollars or do a lot of work. I just have to accept the fact that I'm a sinner,
repent, and rest on that. That's all I have. Now that I look back, it seems
so simple, but at that time I couldn't get it."

Young Trev Alberts was a thinker, and even after finally understanding that salvation is all of Jesus Christ and none of himself, he
struggled.

"Immediately after it happened," he recalls, "I think for the next
week or so I thought to myself, *It can't be that easy.* And I kept going
back to the fact that this is what the Bible says. I just accepted that.
Accepting Christ at such an early age, I still had to go through all the
parts of growing up. I think there are still times in your life when you
may look back, and you may recommit. Those things have been a natural thing with me. I'm still a sinner."

With the heavy emphasis on family, farming, and faith, it's easy to
see how there wouldn't be any room for football in a family like this. But
as the years wore on, Ken and Linda Alberts relented and let their boys
compete. Neither parent had been active in sports and initially declared
athletics off-limits. Finally, during Troy's junior year, they thought, *Well,
maybe it's not a bad thing. We should let him play.* So Troy got started
in sports, and Trev was able to play competitively shortly after that.

There is no bitterness in Trev Alberts regarding the late start he got
in sports because of his parents' initial reluctance to allow their boys to
get involved. Clearly, he knew that what his parents were offering him
and his siblings was a remarkable gift—a close-knit family that worked
hard and loved God.

"My family was so close-knit because of all the stuff we did together," he recalls. "I'm close to my mom and sister, but I'd say my brother
and dad even more so. We went through so much together. We were
always together. We had breakfast, lunch, dinner—everything together,
regardless of who was the last one home. If I had basketball practice till
6:30, then no one ate till I got home. And that's just the way it was. I
didn't know anyone had anything else different. At the time, I didn't
realize the impact.

"As a kid I would see my dad work and just think, 'Wow, I can't wait till the day I can do that.' I always thought my dad was so strong and so tough. He was about 5 feet 10 and about 185 pounds," says the 6 feet 4, 245-pound Trev, chuckling at the irony.

The Alberts family had another characteristic that set them apart from the way many families exist today. They didn't have a television.

"I remember days in the wintertime when we didn't have a lot of work to do. We'd just build a fire, and we'd sit around the fire and we'd talk, or we'd listen to an Iowa football game together on the radio. That's just how it always was."

That close-knit family feeling extended to the church. Everyone went together, and they went every Sunday, no matter the farming chores that waited. "I don't care if we had three-quarters of the corn to pick in the middle of January, and Sunday was a beautiful day; we would not be working. We didn't mow the lawn; Mom didn't do the laundry. That's just the way it was."

To the Alberts family, Sunday was a special day—a set-apart day. Respect for Sunday was such an ingrained belief that when it came time to choose a college to attend, Trev Alberts found that one college coach's attitude toward Sundays played a big role in his decision. It may be one of the few times in recruiting history that a player was influenced to attend a certain school because of how the coach treated the Lord's Day.

Since the Alberts family loved Iowa football, it seemed to be a no-brainer that when Trev turned out to be an outstanding high school football player, he would turn to Iowa City for his college career. In fact, only the University of Iowa and Iowa State actively recruited him. So, true to what everyone expected, Trev made an oral commitment to attend Iowa and spend the next four or five years as a Hawkeye.

But then, in a surprise move, he got a feeler from out of state.

"I got a call from Nebraska, and the coaching staff asked me for a recruiting visit," Alberts recalls. "Actually, they offered me a scholarship before I even went. So, even though I had committed orally to Iowa, I decided, 'Let's just go out there and see what they have.'"

What they have in Lincoln, Nebraska, is Coach Tom Osborne, a man who is noted for his Christian faith and his concern and care for his players. And, oh, yes, he also has a rather remarkable record as a football coach. At that point he hadn't led Nebraska to a national collegiate championship, but everyone knew it was just a matter of time till it would happen.

"I was able to sit down with my mom and dad and listen to Coach Osborne talk. We asked him about his faith. He said stuff like, 'We don't practice on Sunday. That's the Lord's Day.' Things like that I didn't find anywhere else in college football.

"He had a book out called *More Than Winning,* and he told us that if we wanted to read it, we'd have to buy it, because it's an NCAA violation for him to give it to me. We bought the book, and we read it, and we came to the conclusion, as a family, that the best place for me to grow athletically and spiritually was Nebraska. So that's where I went."

It's no secret that recruiting pitches can sometimes be nothing more than empty promises, with coaches promising everything the NCAA allows to sign a recruit. But Coach Osborne wasn't blowing smoke. He kept his vow to Trev Alberts about the Sunday thing. "True to his word," Alberts says, "for five years we never had anything on Sunday: no meetings, no practice, no anything. That allowed me to go to church in Lincoln."

Not only did Trev Alberts go to church as a Christian in Lincoln, but he also went "to town" as a football player. Although he had been recruited by just two Division I-A schools, it wasn't long before every other coach in the nation knew about him. After redshirting in the 1989 season, he began to make his mark during his freshman year of eligibility. Playing as a reserve linebacker in 1990, Alberts was named the Big Eight Conference Defensive Freshman of the Year.

Though only a reserve, he had 26 tackles, 4 sacks, and 1 recovered fumble. In one game, against Iowa State, he had 3 sacks for a total of 27 yards. He lettered that year for Nebraska, enabling him to letter all four years in Lincoln.

Alberts's sophomore year also saw him coming off the bench to spell the regulars. From his part-time outside linebacker position, he put up some impressive numbers: 53 tackles, 7 sacks, and 3 fumbles recovered. Finally, in an exciting Orange Bowl game against Miami, he had 5 tackles and an interception. Miami won, 22–0, but people began to notice the Nebraska reserve.

Alberts became a mainstay of the Nebraska defense his junior and senior years. During an impressive senior season, he led the Huskers with 96 tackles, including 47 solo stops. Add to that his 21 tackles for a loss, 15 sacks (tying the school record), 38 quarterback pressures, and 3 forced fumbles, and you have the makings of the best linebacker in the land.

Coach Osborne told reporters during Alberts's sensational final year, "We've had some great players at that position over the years, but Trev has probably surpassed what every one of them has done. I haven't seen every player in the country at his position, but I can't imagine any of them being any better than Trev."

The respect in this situation went both ways. Alberts looks back on his years at Nebraska with fondness—and credits Coach Osborne for that feeling. "It may happen elsewhere in the nation, but I can't think of any other program, at that level, where this could happen. I remember every week a verse was put in front of us, on the board, in front of every single kid. Coach Osborne never took the stance of saying, you have to be this kind of Christian. He said, 'Whatever you believe, do it to the fullest.' He would put verses up in front of us, and I've carried that to this day. When I have my ups and downs in football, many times I think back to some of the things he put up on the board. The Bible talks about everything. You can apply it to anything that happens in life. He could always find that for us."

But all was not problem-free for Alberts during his final year as a college football player. Because he was a fifth-year player, Alberts had gone into the season with his college degree in hand, and he was working on his master's degree during the season. His work in speech communications would come in handy sooner than he expected, for events unfolded during the last game of the season that would have spillover effects during his first year in the pros.

In the final season game of 1993, the Cornhuskers were playing number sixteen Oklahoma. On the ninth play of the game, Alberts dislocated his right elbow trying to make a tackle. He left the game, and his status was uncertain for the big game against number one Florida State in the Orange Bowl. Trev Alberts had never missed a football game because of an injury, but that streak was in jeopardy.

Team physicians put the arm in a cast for about a month and let him begin rehabilitation after that. One of the Nebraska team physicians later declared that he had never seen an injury like Trev's in his twenty-two years on the job.

It was a tough injury for his teammates to accept. "Everybody's head dropped for a second when Trev got hurt," said fellow linebacker Dwayne Harris. "But that didn't last long. We knew we had to do it for Trev because he's carried us this year."

Meanwhile, Alberts showed calm maturity. He could have been bitter, but instead told reporters, "I hope I'll be back for the Orange Bowl, but I'll let this happen any day if that's what it takes for us to win. Getting injured is part of the game of football. We're 11-0 and have our first chance since 1983 to play for the national championship. I know I was part of it, and I hope I can still be a big part of it by just being around the locker room and at practice."

As it turned out, Alberts was indeed a big part of the Orange Bowl—and not just in the locker room. His arm recovered enough for him to play on January 1 against Florida State. The Seminoles were after their first national championship under Bobby Bowden, and the Cornhuskers wanted to show the world that *they* were number one.

It didn't take Alberts long to assert himself on the field. In the first half, he was a major player in helping the Huskers to a 7-6 lead as he pestered the Seminoles Heisman Trophy–winning quarterback Charlie Ward all half, including two sacks of the future NBA player.

The second half was another tight battle. Florida State scored first to take a 15-7 lead. But when Nebraska's Lawrence Phillips scored to make the score 15-13, it was still anyone's game. After the TD, the Huskers opted to go for two points, hoping that they would just need one more score after that to win. Tommie Frazier rolled out to the right to pass, but couldn't find a receiver. He headed for the end zone, but was bumped out of bounds at the 1-yard line. The score remained 15-13.

With four minutes to go in the game, Nebraska got that other score they were looking for when Byron Bennett booted a 27-yard field goal. The men from Lincoln led, 16-15.

But Florida State wasn't done. Charlie Ward led the Seminoles downfield before kicker Scott Bentley nailed an easy 13-yard field goal with 20 seconds left.

That was sufficient time as Nebraska, helped by some unusual calls by the officials, marched into field goal range of their own. With one second left, Bennett attempted a 45-yard kick, but it sailed left. Florida State, and not Nebraska, became the national champions.

In this dramatic first day of 1994, Trev Alberts's career at Nebraska ended. But his football legacy to Husker fans continued in two special ways. First, Alberts was the first Cornhusker to win the Butkus Award, as the top college linebacker in the nation. Second, at least three sets of Columbus, Nebraska, parents chose to honor the Cornhuskers' linebacker by naming their sons after him. One parent, the mother of Trev Michael Rawhouser, summed up the feelings of the boys' moms and dads. "If he [Alberts] wasn't so neat, I wouldn't have named Trev Michael after him. He's a real positive role model."

Of course, NFL scouts are not looking primarily for role models during their draft of college football players. They want men who are quick, strong, smart, and talented. If they happen to be respectable people too, then so much the better. With Trev Alberts, the Indianapolis Colts got all those things. The selection of Alberts, however, surprised many of the experts, and even Alberts was surprised.

"I was never contacted by the Colts, almost to the point where it seemed like they didn't want me. But apparently, it was a scheme of theirs to make sure that no one knew they were interested in me so they could take me."

And take him they did. The Colts had already made one first-round pick, taking running back Marshall Faulk. Then, with their next pick— the fifth selection overall, a pick obtained in a trade with the Rams— they called Trev Alberts's name. The big Husker linebacker, at home in Cedar Falls with his family, got a phone call from the Colts' organization just before it was announced on TV. Alberts was so surprised that he doubted the caller's words.

"I didn't know if I should believe the guy, because they hadn't announced yet that there was a trade. I knew the Rams had the fifth pick, and this man was telling me that I was taken with the fifth pick. So there was a little conflict there, but as time went on, and they showed it on TV, it became more real to me."

With that conflict resolved, another brewed right away. Typical of the hoopla and second-guessing associated with NFL draft day, ESPN-TV, which was carrying the draft live, was including the commentary of draft analyst Mel Kiper. And when he heard that Indianapolis had selected a linebacker with their second high pick, Kiper was shocked. He, as did many other experts, expected Indy to select Trent Dilfer from Fresno State.

Immediately, Kiper went airborne on the air. He berated the Colts for picking Alberts, railing on them for not picking up what he thought they needed—a top-ranked quarterback. Soon Indianapolis general manager Bill Tobin was on the screen, hotly defending his choice. It was not exactly a friendly exchange between two gentlemen.

Alberts, both an innocent bystander and the center of attention in this whole thing, was philosophical about the goings-on. "I don't think I was necessarily the center of the controversy. I think it was more the selection of a linebacker over what you would consider a franchise quarterback. The Colts had a definite direction that they wanted to head—building a solid defense as well as a running game—and they needed an experienced quarterback. They told me that Trent Dilfer would take some time to develop. And frankly, the Colts couldn't wait another two or three years."

In retrospect, it appears that the Colts were right. Into Alberts's and Dilfer's second year in the league, as Dilfer was still struggling to get established in Tampa Bay, the Colts were only one pass short of going to the Super Bowl behind seasoned quarterback Jim Harbaugh. And Alberts had become a key part of the Colts' line.

As good as the pick seems now, the positive results were slow in coming. And a lot of that is the result of that injury Alberts had suffered back in November 1993.

After drafting the young linebacker, Colt coach Ted Marchibroda gave a high compliment: "What I like about Trev is that . . . his motor is going all the time. He's a 60-minute player who plays sideline to sideline." But in the first half of his first exhibition game as a pro, Alberts reinjured his right elbow. Now he would become a less-than-30-minute player.

Three weeks after the injury, noted sports physician Frank Jobe repaired the offending elbow. It looked like Trev's first season was a washout.

"It's certainly had its ups and downs," Alberts said of his truncated first year that included controversy on ESPN, reporting late to training camp as negotiations bogged down on his first contract, and NFL lawyers then reviewing the signed contract to be sure it adhered to new league rules in 1994. "It's like any football game. You have great plays, and you have some bad ones. It's a roller coaster."

To avoid having the season be one that rolled downhill completely, Alberts found a way to use his Nebraska education while waiting for his arm to heal. And irony of ironies, he put his communications training to work for ESPN, the network of Mel Kiper. While on the mend, Alberts worked weekend college games for ESPN2.

Smiling at the recollection, Alberts jokes about his time with the sports network. "That situation was funny. It was like, 'The guy can't play football, but you know what, he can really come out and talk.' I had a lot of people ask me if I had ever run into that Mel Kiper guy. I didn't, but we all had some good jokes about it.

"Seriously, the ESPN people were really good to me. I really enjoyed it because I could take a step back and still be involved. It was a good release for me to take my mind off the injury."

The injury episode was also a time of reflection for Alberts. "That wasn't something I was prepared for. Up to that point, I had never missed a game in my life. But I firmly believe that God has a reason for everything.

"That time was needed in my life. I had had such a storybook, dream career at Nebraska. Everything just went right for me. The injury forced me to step back and take a good look at what was really important. Maybe I didn't handle some of the success the best at the time. Maybe it's just God's way of saying, 'Hey, wait a minute. I just want to remind you that I'm still in control.' "

With his lesson learned, Alberts returned to the game sooner than his doctors expected. Dr. Jobe had told Alberts that the usual rehab for his kind of injury is a year. But three months after the surgery, the elbow appeared to be right. The quick-healing athlete was ready to play. So, on Sunday, November 27, Trev Alberts made his belated NFL regular-season debut against the New England Patriots. Alberts had six tackles, including one sack of Patriots quarterback Drew Bledsoe.

"Trev did a good job," Marchibroda remarked after the game. "You knew he was on the football field. He was productive. He had a few errors, which is understandable. But overall, we're happy with his performance."

There was no storybook ending to 1994. Although Alberts remained healthy, his presence was not enough to push the Colts into the playoffs.

But 1995 was another story.

Jim Harbaugh was supposed to be replaced by Craig Erickson. Ted Marchibroda was supposed to be overmatched by the bright, young coaches. And the defensive line was not supposed to have the right components. All in all, the Colts were not supposed to be where they were in January—in the playoffs and pointing toward the Super Bowl. And without Marshall Faulk, who was supposed to be the lone bright spot.

Yet the overachieving Colts were right there at the end, battling Pittsburgh for the AFC title and a trip to the Super Bowl.

For Alberts, that great turnaround for the Colts has been his NFL highlight. "Being a part of getting this thing turned around has been great," Alberts says. "I heard a lot of people saying a lot of things about the players and their attitude and stuff. We may not have the most talent in the NFL, but we've got forty-eight guys who will fight you and fight you for a whole game. And that's been fun. We haven't totally turned the corner yet. Going to Nebraska, I knew that whether I was there or not, they would be going places. I looked at coming to Indianapolis as a great challenge to go somewhere that was still turning it around."

Trev started the first three games that year before becoming backup to defensive end Tony Bennett. He watched and cheered as the defense jelled, climaxing with a dramatic 10–7 win over Kansas City—a victory that put the Colts at the door of the Super Bowl. Heading into the AFC championship game against Pittsburgh, Alberts knew that the Colts needed to take advantage of their underdog status. "The worst thing for this team would be if everybody on TV said, 'The Colts will beat the Steelers.'"

Nobody did, but the Colts nearly did, losing 20–16 to end a remarkable season.

To this football player, family is still important. And even after two years in the NFL, that family belief in a God-prescribed day off is still a strong factor. In fact, Trev thinks the major downside of playing in the NFL is that the games are held on Sunday. "One of the things that I really enjoyed about Nebraska was that even though we played every Saturday, every Sunday I was able to go to Hollywood Heights Bible Chapel and had great fellowship there. It's just not feasible on Sundays. You're looking from June to January. You go to chapel before the game, but it's not the same. I really miss the fellowship and getting together on a weekly basis. That's been kind of difficult."

You'd think playing in below-zero temperatures or being blocked by 300-pound linemen or taking a beating week after week or the tedium of practice or some other more normal football difficulty would pose the biggest problem for a relatively new NFL player. Not so.

To Trev Alberts, a belief more fundamental than how to tackle or avoid a blocker takes precedent. It seems that no matter how comfortable he becomes as an NFL player, he'll never fully agree with when the games are played. Even if the Colts get into the Super Bowl, he would probably wish it was never on a Sunday.

Q & A WITH TREV ALBERTS

Q: *What do you do during the season to stay spiritually sharp?*
Trev: During the season, it has to be an individual thing. The demands on your time are so incredible. It's unbelievable. I'm fortunate enough to have a girlfriend who is interested in Bible study, and we are able to do that together. There's just not a lot of opportunity.

Q: *What is your favorite Scripture passage?*
Trev: "I can do all things through Christ who strengthens me." I'm one of those guys who . . . I have talent or I wouldn't be here, but a lot of my success is just based on just fighting through it and finding a way to get it done. And that's always, when I'm down, I just keep remembering to keep fighting and believe and have faith.

I'd be in big trouble if I didn't have faith in the Lord.

Q: *What kind of Bible reading regimen do you keep?*
Trev: I try to make it a habit regardless of whether it's only two or three minutes a day. I try to at least expose myself to something every day. My parents I know still have the same routine.

Q: *How do you use football for the Lord?*
Trev: There's a reason I'm with the Indianapolis Colts, and I think I just always tried to keep the big picture and realize my position, the smallness in the really big scheme of life and the importance of it. And try to remember that football's a game and that shouldn't be the sole reason that I'm on the earth. Hopefully, I can use football in some small way to serve the Lord if that's His will.

Certainly He's blessed me in a lot of things in football. So I believe that's what I ought to be doing. But I think keeping in perspective who I am on this earth in comparison to the great God we have has allowed me to keep things in focus.

Q: *Has your success as a pro athlete caused any struggles with feelings of pride?*
Trev: I would say that my first year I might have taken some things for granted. Sometimes you fall into the trap of "Hey, I play in the NFL." It just doesn't take long before you need to be humbled again. I'd like to think it hasn't.

If you knew my family, you would know that the minute they would ever detect that NFL pride, it would change pretty quickly.

Mark Brunell
Stepping Up

VITAL STATISTICS

Born September 17, 1970, in Santa Maria, California
6 feet, 217 pounds
College: University of Washington
Position: Quarterback
1996 team: Jacksonville Jaguars

CAREER HIGHLIGHTS

- Led Jaguars to the franchise's first-ever win (1995) with a fourth-quarter drive against the Houston Oilers
- Holds team records for passes (48), completions (30), and passing yards (302)
- Most Valuable Player in the Rose Bowl (1991)
- Passed for 5,893 yards during high school career

WARMING UP

Though he played high school football outside L.A. and San Francisco, his exploits did get enough attention to attract the notice of that school he always dreamed of playing at, USC. In fact, Mark Brunell was recruited by most of the Pacific-10 schools.

The problem with USC was that although they were interested in Brunell, he was not at the top of their list. "I really like the southern California schools. I liked UCLA. I liked USC."

More than that—and this would be a theme that would recur occasionally throughout his career—Mark Brunell was not the number one quarterback prospect of any of those schools. "I was second or third on their lists as far as quarterbacks that they wanted," he explains.

"It was tough at first," he recalls, "realizing that these schools wanted someone else."

They would end up paying for that judgment call when Brunell chose Pac-10 rival Washington.

Mark Brunell

I f you were a NASCAR driver, and you looked in your rearview mirror and saw Mark Brunell sneaking up behind you, you might just as well wave him on past. He's going to pass you eventually anyway.

Brunell, of course, is no threat to the good ol' boys on the asphalt tracks, but on the football field he seems to be perfectly capable of taking care of himself. Mark Brunell may sometimes start off in second place, but more often than not, in one way or another, he'll end up in first place looking back.

It happened after high school, when it came time to be recruited. It happened in college. It happened at Jacksonville in the NFL.

Now, it didn't happen with the NFL's Green Bay Packers. But that's perfectly OK with Brunell. Because, as we will see, Mark knows how to step up when adversity comes and make the most of a situation.

Consider how he turned his high school location into a plus. Hometown was a three-hour drive north of the Los Angeles area; Santa Maria, to be exact. All the publicity goes to L.A. area athletes, but Mark developed into an outstanding high school football player at Santa Maria and caught the attention of the southern California schools anyway.

Though he grew up in Santa Maria, Mark had deep roots in the L.A. area: his father was an L.A. product. Dad grew up in the city, and he participated in college athletics there. Plus the elder Brunell, who was Mark's JV football and varsity baseball coach, was a huge Los Angeles Dodgers fan. And so Mark's football dreams focused southward toward the City of Angels. He envisioned taking the field in the maroon and gold of the University of Southern California Trojans.

But before it was time to decide on a college, Mark and the other Brunell men enjoyed football—and a lot of other sports. Not only did Dad play and then turn to coaching, but his two sons couldn't get enough of the action. "If we weren't playing basketball, we were playing baseball," Mark recalls. "We were always doing something with sports."

But it wasn't all games all the time for the Brunells. Mark's parents also made sure there was a spiritual influence in their lives. After trying a couple of churches, the Brunells finally decided on a Baptist church, where Mark found someone he considers one of his most important influences as a teenager.

It was his youth pastor, Tim Petty. "He was a football coach also, so I really respected him and looked up to him." Brunell also liked the fact that the youth group was very active. "We had one of those youth groups that was always doing stuff. We went to camps, and we had Monday night get-togethers."

But as Brunell now understands, going to church and being a dedicated Christian can be two entirely different things. "I was very involved in my church, but I was not very committed," he admits. "I went to all the events, and I was in all the meetings, but I wasn't committed as a Christian. I was really only a Christian one day of the week and that was Sunday."

The rest of the week, he was more interested in pleasing his friends than in pleasing God. "I wasn't willing to take a stand among my friends and really show them what I believed. I think it was from fear of what they might think. I just wasn't willing to live that part of my life around my high school friends. It just wasn't cool."

What Brunell lacked in dedication to God he certainly made up in dedication to his sport. At St. Joseph High School in Santa Maria, Brunell had an incredible football career. During his years at the school, where his dad served as a PE teacher, coach, and athletic director, Brunell passed for an amazing 5,893 yards and fired 41 touchdown passes. It was no wonder that during his graduation year he was named by *The Sporting News* as one of its Top 100 high school football players in the country.

When he wasn't playing football, Brunell played enough basketball to become a second-team all-league selection and enough baseball to be named the league MVP his senior year and a four-time all-league pick. However, because he played in a school outside the L.A. and San Francisco areas, he didn't attract as much attention as some other college hopefuls. "We didn't get the media coverage that we would have liked, being on the central coast," Brunell explains.

But he did attract the notice of that school he always dreamed of playing at, USC. In fact, Brunell was recruited by most of the Pacific-10 schools.

The problem with USC was that although they were interested in Brunell, he was not at the top of their list. "I really like the southern California schools. I liked UCLA. I liked USC."

More than that—and this would be a theme that would recur occasionally throughout his career—Mark Brunell was not the number one quarterback prospect of any of those schools. "I was second or third on their lists as far as quarterbacks that they wanted," he explains.

"It was tough at first," he recalls, "realizing that these schools wanted someone else."

They would end up paying for that judgment call.

Far up the coast in Seattle was a coach who really liked what he saw in Mark Brunell. Don James and his staff had a different view of the hot, young quarterback. "With Washington, I was number one, and that made me feel pretty good." He felt even better after making his recruiting visit to the land of the Huskies.

"I took my trip to Washington, and I really fell in love with it." Soon his name was on a letter of intent. He had survived his first brush with being the number two (or lower) quarterback on the depth chart. He would go to Washington as the top recruit at QB, assured that after a redshirt freshman year, the job would be his.

But before Brunell was able to deliver on his promise as the quarterback of the future at Washington, someone with a great deal more authority than Don James got his attention.

Brunell's introduction to college was accompanied by the usual feelings that many freshmen develop in their first year away from home. Besides the homesickness, which Brunell understandably had from being so far from his central California home, he also developed that anything-goes attitude that destroys many eighteen-year-olds.

"When I got up to college, I was feeling pretty good that I was on my own. I could make my own decisions. My mom had told me, 'Son, it's really important that you find a church. Meet people and get involved.'

"I had told her, 'Sure, Mom.' But I never really did it.

"It was a whole new environment. I didn't have to go to bed till I wanted to. I was on my own program. This led to kind of a rebellion stage, and then I just totally rejected everything I knew about Christ and my faith. For the first year, this was what was going on. I would still call myself a Christian. I would still go to the FCA [Fellowship of Christian Athletes] now and then, but as far as serving God, I wasn't doing that at all."

By now, after going through an entire year of working out with the Huskies and becoming firmly entrenched in the scene at the University of Washington, those dreams of playing for a school like Southern Cal had vanished. For Brunell, USC was a gridiron opponent, a team that stood in the way of getting to the Rose Bowl.

"I didn't think anything good could come out of USC," Brunell says of this time in his life.

But it did. And it had less to do with football than it had to do with Brunell's decision to make an end run around his commitment to Christ in search of college good times. It had to do with a challenge given from a fellow Californian.

At the end of his freshman year, a fellow player received an invitation to hear the USC chaplain, who was in town. The Husky player invited Brunell. "We both thought, 'Hey, why don't we go listen to this guy!' "

The chaplain's name was Tom Sirotnak, a former football player himself. He has since gone on to write a book called *Warriors*, in which he challenges men to stand up for their faith in Jesus Christ.

"My friend and I went and listened to Tom. He just spoke right at us. It was as if we were the only two in there. My friend was in a situation similar to mine. He went to church in high school, but when he got to college, he drifted off like I did.

"But that night we both decided that we were off the mark, and we had to straighten out our lives. God did something that night. We decided to make Him number one. No partying, no more living for ourselves. It was just a total turnaround." A kid who was not willing to risk his popularity in high school to let people know he was a Christian was now willing to commit every part of his life to God.

"Like I said, I didn't think anything good could come out of USC, but I was wrong."

A representative of the school that didn't want Mark Brunell to be their number one quarterback had suddenly become very influential in setting him on course to make God number one in his life. Of course, that would not be the only time Brunell would be involved with USC. There were four years of gridiron meetings laying ahead.

Brunell, though, would face those meetings as a changed young man. Helping Brunell with this new, more godly path was the teammate who had joined him that night to hear Sirotnak. "What was very good was that I had someone to do this with me. Someone who was on the football team. Todd Bridge became my roommate and he's my best friend now. We went through it together. It was great. We spent time in the Word together. That was really the turning point in my life spiritually. It was an exciting time."

Exciting times lay ahead for Brunell on the football field as well. After redshirting his freshman year and playing behind Cary Conklin the next, Brunell was handed the ball and told to lead the Huskies as a redshirt sophomore (his third year at Washington). Brunell and the vastly improved Huskies then achieved what Brunell considers his highlight moment for the Big Purple. And wouldn't you know it, this highlight came against that school of his dreams, that school whose chaplain changed his life: the University of Southern California.

By now, Southern Cal had picked up perhaps the most noted college quarterback in the land. His name was Todd Marinovich, and he had been groomed from infancy by his father to one day become a quarterback. In the matchup of Marinovich and Brunell—two athletes who would have been battling for QB duties had Brunell gone to USC—Brunell won in monstrous fashion. The Huskies shut out the Trojans 31–0, the worst Pac-10 defeat for USC in thirty years.

"That was a highlight," Brunell recalls. "We were kind of the little guys, and USC was the big-time team. It kind of turned things around for our program. We went to the Rose Bowl that year and the following two years."

In each of Brunell's four years on the field for the Huskies, the team went to a bowl game. During his first year of suiting up, they played in the Freedom Bowl, and from 1991 through 1993, they went to the Rose Bowl.

For Brunell, the first Rose Bowl game was the best. Washington traveled to Pasadena and defeated Iowa, 46-34, as Brunell won the game's most valuable player award. For now, Mark Brunell was the top gun at the helm of Washington's offense, and the Huskies were the top team in the Pacific-10. It may not have been what was expected when he took his considerable skills north a couple of years earlier, but he was beginning to develop a reputation for overcoming whatever adversity was coming his way and ending up on top. A reputation for stepping up when needed.

But then the roof caved in. Or rather his right knee.

On the tenth day of Washington's spring practice, Brunell, who was wearing a green vest to signal to his teammates that he was not to be hit, was nailed from the side.

A pall fell over the Huskies as they stood over their injured comrade. "It was like a funeral," said Coach James. "I could have cried."

Touted as a possible number one team for the 1991 season, Washington had a solid defense anchored by Steve Emtman, and they had Rose Bowl MVP Mark Brunell returning for his junior year.

Major ligaments in Brunell's right knee were damaged, and it looked as if he would be out for the entire season to come. Five months after surgery and following extensive rehabilitation, Brunell was ready to play again. He had missed the first two games; for game three he would have only limited action.

While he was out he had lost his number one job to Billy Joe Hobert. Although Hobert did not have the footspeed that Brunell showed, he did have a rifle arm. The two would divide time behind the center during the rest of the season. Behind Hobert and Brunell, the Huskies made it back to the Rose Bowl after the 1991 season. Despite a partial year for Brunell, the Huskies finished undefeated and shared the 1991 national championship with the Miami Hurricanes.

When the 1992 season rolled around, the Huskies were again picked to be one of the top teams in the country. Although Emtman had turned pro, Washington still had tailback Napoleon Kaufman and tackle Lincoln Kennedy to bolster the strong quarterback duo of Hobert and Brunell. Coach James had decided before the season began that the signal callers would share the duties running the offense because he didn't see enough difference between the two to make a definitive call.

But as the season wore on and Washington seemed to be steaming toward another undefeated season, a couple of setbacks slowed them down. First, Hobert, who had seen Brunell recapture the starting job at quarterback, was suspended from the team for taking questionable loans. Not only did he blow the $50,000 in loans, but he also was involved in talk of gambling.

Once again, through both his own effort and the failure of his fellow quarterback, Brunell had stepped up to the front. Under Brunell's leadership, the Huskies finished 9–2 and went to their third straight Rose Bowl. This time, Washington lost to Michigan, 38–31.

All that was left for Brunell now was the interminable wait between the end of the season and the NFL draft. He wondered where he would be drafted, yet really it didn't matter. But his wife, Stacy, had expressed a preference—anywhere but Green Bay's chilly Lambeau Field. Before the draft, Stacy prayed, "I'll go anywhere, just don't put us in Green Bay, Wisconsin."

Mark and Stacy were both athletes at Washington. She ran track and cross country, and the two of them met in what must be considered a logical—if not romantic—place: the college weight room at the leg extension machine. And now, three years later, they were about to get a payoff for all of the time Mark had spent pumping up.

When draft day rolled around, Mark and Stacy gathered at Stacy's parents' house in Issaquah, a town east of Seattle. Mark had been told by some that he would be picked in the second or third round. But he heard nothing during the first day of the draft. Finally, on the second day, he got the call. "I didn't go until the second day in the fifth round. At the time, it was really frustrating. And then to go to Green Bay, of all places."

Yes, it was the Packers who picked up this kid from central California. He and Stacy were headed to the last place in the NFL she wanted to go.

There might be a couple of very good reasons that a promising quarterback and his wife might not want to go there. For the quarterback it might be Brett Favre, who was coming into his own as a fine quarterback. For the wife—well, let's just say that Green Bay isn't exactly the West Coast.

But remember, this is the guy who wasn't able to go to a southern California school and did fine. This was a guy who lost his number one spot because of an injury and worked his way back to the top. Surely he could turn the Green Bay situation into a winner.

If that means he came storming on the scene to unseat Favre and send him into early retirement, it didn't happen. If it means he used his Green Bay experience to help him become a very good NFL quarterback, then that's exactly what happened.

Brunell now says, "As it turned out, Green Bay was the perfect place for me. I was coached by some great coaches like Mike Holmgren. I was in a great system that taught me about the game of pro football."

The coaches and Green Bay management were "really good people," Brunell says. "They took care of me as a player."

It was also a time of spiritual growth for Brunell. "I met a lot of good friends there. Played with Reggie White. We had a great Bible study. Bryce Paup was on this team. There were a lot of guys who were big-time pro athletes but the priority in their lives is Jesus Christ."

In April 1995, though, Brunell was traded from the Packers to the brand-new Jacksonville Jaguars, in Jacksonville's first-ever trade. The Jaguars already had two other quarterbacks, from the college and expansion drafts, Andre Ware and Steve Beuerlein. Ware and Beuerlein were slated to be the team's one-two punch behind center. It appeared certain that Brunell would again be standing on the sideline, waiting for a shot at playing.

Yet as he has done throughout his career, Brunell stepped to the front. First, Ware was dropped from the squad, moving Beuerlein and Brunell up a notch. Then, after the season began, Brunell showed that he could both pass and run. When Beuerlein was sidelined in the second game of the season with a sprained right knee, Brunell stepped in from the wings.

On October 1, 1995, he led the Jaguars to their first-ever regular season victory when he fired a 15-yard touchdown pass to Desmond Howard with 63 seconds left in a game with Houston for a 17–16 win. "They put me in during the fourth quarter, and we won," Brunell recalls. "They gave me the starting job after that, and I kept it for the rest of the year."

After his first few games as the team's top quarterback, Brunell had also become the team's top runner. That standard didn't last all season, but he did finish second on the team in rushing with 480 yards on 67 carries.

The biggest game for Brunell, though, came the week after the

Houston win. The Pittsburgh Steelers were in town for a contest with the upstart Jaguars. The Steelers were struggling, having lost two of their previous three contests. They were not playing anything like they would play several weeks later when they earned a spot in the Super Bowl.

Against the Steelers, Brunell passed for 189 yards to lead the Jaguars to a 20–16 win over the black and gold. It was the first time since 1968 that an expansion team had won back-to-back games.

"Beating Pittsburgh was my highlight of that first year," Brunell says. "It was our first win at home in the regular season. We were the David and they were the Goliath. It was really an exciting day."

A week later, the Jaguars had another exciting day, although the end result wasn't as thrilling. The Chicago Bears came into Jacksonville, and the Jaguars gave them all they could handle. When the dust cleared, the Bears had won, 30–27. In that game, Brunell set team records for passes (48), completions (30), yards (302), and touchdowns (3).

In the seven weeks since the season began, Brunell had established himself as the top quarterback on the Jaguars. By the time the season ended, he had climbed to seventh in the AFC in passing efficiency. His 346 attempts and 201 completions put him near the top for expansion quarterbacks in NFL history.

No one could have known when he was traded from the Packers how well his first year with Jacksonville would go, least of all Brunell. "I didn't really know what to expect going to an expansion team," he says, looking back. "It was a great opportunity to play, and hopefully to start. But it was very exciting in that it was all brand-new. You never know what to expect from an expansion team. You figure you're going to take your lumps for a couple of years. But this year I got the starting job and was able to play a lot, so it worked out just as I had hoped."

A lot has changed for Mark Brunell since those days when his dream of playing football at UCLA or USC ended and he left for Washington. But at each point, he has learned how to step up to the next level, both athletically and spiritually. And now that he is a veteran NFL quarterback, he knows that beyond his own dreams are some other responsibilities.

"Being in the NFL has changed me. I think what has really changed me is that God has molded me into the person I think He wants me to be. I think pro athletes have an incredible responsibility. We are called to be stewards of the talent God has given us. It's an incredible platform, and it has caused me to grow up and mature."

To step up, one might say. Which is what Mark Brunell has done, no matter where he calls the signals.

Q & A WITH MARK BRUNELL

Q: *What is your feeling about the future of the Jaguars?*
Mark: We have a good feeling about ourselves. We obviously have a lot of work to do. But we've grown, and we're a better team than we were in the beginning. We just have to take this into the off-season and get ready for next year.

Q: *What is your favorite Bible passage?*
Mark: It's Jeremiah 29:11: "'For I know the plans I have for you,'" declares the Lord, "'plans to prosper you and not to harm you, plans to give you hope and a future.'"

Q: *How do you view the concept of being a role model?*
Mark: Pro football players are so much in the spotlight. People are watching you, especially kids. And you're their role model. You're their example, and if you're doing the things you shouldn't be doing, they're going to see that. I think God has given us so much responsibility, and I think we have to live up to that.

Trent Dilfer
The Dilfer Difference

VITAL STATISTICS

Born March 13, 1972, in Santa Cruz, California
6 feet 4, 235 pounds
College: Fresno State University
Position: Quarterback
1996 team: Tampa Bay Buccaneers

CAREER HIGHLIGHTS

- Completed 24 passes for 249 yards in 1995 overtime win against Minnesota
- Chosen in first round of 1994 college draft (sixth player drafted)
- Selected college All-American twice (1992, 1993)
- Holds NCAA record for most consecutive passes thrown without an interception (271)

WARMING UP

Trent Dilfer was on his way, and he thought he knew how to go in style. "I really thought I was hot stuff. When your ego gets involved with drugs and alcohol, it's a deadly combination, and that's what happened to me."

What else began to happen in Dilfer's life during his freshman year was something an observer would least expect at this time. Trent Dilfer, the loose-living, heavy-drinking, self-centered college stud quarterback, was also going around Fresno talking about Jesus.

Ironically, he was talking about the humble carpenter as a way to feed a proud quarterback's ego.

Trent Dilfer

Visit any high school in the country that has produced a great athlete, and you'll probably find the hallways full of people who are willing to brag about everybody's best friend Lefty and what a great guy he was.

Trent Dilfer is afraid it isn't that way with him and good old Aptos High in Santa Cruz, California. It's not that Dilfer wasn't a great athlete.

He was. In golf, he was all-league. In basketball, he was league player of the year as a senior. In football, he once threw for five touchdowns in one game. As a senior, he passed for 1,126 yards and 15 touchdowns while rushing for 400 yards and seven more TDs.

And it's not that he wasn't a good student.

He was that too. In the classroom, he graduated with a 3.9 grade point average.

The problem, according to no less an expert than Trent Dilfer himself, was that he just wasn't a very good person.

"You go back to my high school," Dilfer begins, "and there's not a whole lot of people who have a lot of nice things to say about me. Depending on what season it was dictated who liked me. During the football season, the football fans liked me. During the basketball season, the basketball fans liked me. During the golf season, what few golf fans there were, they liked me."

But what about the teachers? Surely they liked this big, strong, good-looking A student. "Some of them knew my family, so they liked my family. But I don't think many of them liked the way I handled myself. They hated the way I could come into class after missing three straight days and not miss a question on a test."

Dilfer readily admits that the real problem wasn't his brain, it was his ego, which led him to some pretty self-abusive activities. "High school for me is kind of a big blur. I got heavily involved in drinking in high school. I drank because it was the cool thing to do, and I did it in excess because it brought more attention to me."

This was not the Trent Dilfer that his mother and stepfather thought they were raising.

Trent's mother, Marcie, and his stepfather, Frank Lynch (his parents had divorced when he was two, and she married Trent's stepdad about three years later), were both involved in church, and they took him and his sisters along. But for Trent, the message never really hit home.

"I went to church, and I did the Sunday school thing and all that, but I never really understood Christianity," Dilfer explains. "I viewed Christianity as a lot of young people do, and that's as a religion. And a bunch of dos and don'ts and rights and wrongs. I went through elementary school and junior high and high school with off-and-on religious experiences. I prayed the prayer, but for some reason it never really sank in to me. I would do what a Christian was supposed to do for a couple of weeks, and then along would come something that would interest me more, and I'd be off doing that. Usually that was sin."

This inconsistent attitude toward matters of faith, combined with his success on the football field, led Dilfer to seek the spotlight. It was a spotlight he did not want to share with anyone—much less Jesus Christ.

"I always thrived on the spotlight. And I learned new ways to get the spotlight—whether it was drinking a lot or being with a lot of girls, whatever it may be. I was hurting a lot of people in the meantime."

He took his show to Fresno after his inspiring high school career at Aptos. Surprisingly, he received only three college scholarships—Santa Clara, Northern Arizona, and Fresno State. This lack of recruiting attention didn't harm young Dilfer's ego, though. "I thought I was pretty hot stuff, being a quarterback at a major university."

The first year at Fresno was a dream year for an eighteen-year-old kid for whom life is a party. Because he was redshirted, he didn't have to hold back to be ready for Saturday. "All I did was party," he says. "I decided to take all the energy I would put into football and put it into partying."

Year two at Fresno was much more of the same. Yet this time, he was able to play football. When starting quarterback Mark Barsotti suffered a broken leg midway through the season, Dilfer stepped right in and established himself as an outstanding college signal-caller. In nine games, he completed 63 percent of his passes and rushed for five touchdowns.

Trent Dilfer was on his way, and he thought he knew how to go in style. "I really thought I was hot stuff. When your ego gets involved with drugs and alcohol, it's a deadly combination, and that's what happened to me."

What else began to happen in Dilfer's life during his freshman year was something an observer would least expect at this time. Trent Dilfer, the loose-living, heavy-drinking, self-centered college stud quarterback, was also going around Fresno talking about Jesus.

Ironically, he was talking about the humble carpenter as a way to feed a proud quarterback's ego. As Dilfer explains, "My Christian background was surfacing as a way to feed my ego. There was a very strong Fellowship of Christian Athletes program at Fresno, and they got news that I thought I was a Christian—that I grew up in a Christian home. But they didn't really know what I was doing in my life. So they began using my name and my celebrity. They had me out speaking at FCA events and proclaiming the name of Christ at FCA huddles, when the night before I'd go speak, I'd be passed out on my bed with a different girl. It was a very ugly combination."

As the school year ended and Dilfer began making his summer plans, he was asked by the FCA people to attend a summer camp. Knowing that he was not the Christian role model everyone thought he was, Dilfer said yes but decided that he would tell them he was "not in it for the Christian thing, but just to coach some kids how to play football."

But it wasn't as easy as Dilfer thought to ignore the Christian thing. During the two-day prep period for the leaders, about twenty athletes and a couple of leaders prepared spiritually for the incoming campers. "So here I was, a kid who's the farthest thing from a Christian," Trent recalls. "I was so far away from Christ, it's unbelievable. Here I was with nineteen of my peers and a couple of leaders who just love Christ to death, and all they want to do is serve Him.

"Their lifestyles as Christians weren't what I was used to. They were guys who were dedicated to Christ, but they showed it with their actions, not their words. They didn't go around praising Jesus with their mouths and all that. They did it with their lives. The first night I was there, they all sensed what was going on with me, because my heart was very hard, and I was very hard to get along with. They just broke down all the barriers with their love.

"I had no idea what love was. I hadn't been with my family for a long time, so I didn't know what the love of family was. I never had a meaningful relationship [with a girl] in college, so I had no idea what that kind of love was. I didn't love Christ, so I had no idea what that love was. I didn't know Christ, so I didn't understand his love for me.

"But these guys just loved me to death. They prayed with me and for me, and talked to me and laughed with me and cried with me. I saw Christ through them through those first two days."

Before the campers would begin arriving, Trent Dilfer finally made the decision he had only pretended to make before. He knew his parents were praying for him to genuinely trust Jesus Christ. He knew that they had put his life in God's hands and were letting him make his own decisions.

And he knew that he had to be saved. "I came to Jesus and said, 'I can't tell You how sorry I am.' I just confessed everything to Him, and made a decision to trust Him. I told Him that my strength would be in Him instead of the past—the women, the sports, my ego, and alcohol. My decision was for Christ and against the world."

It was the beginning of the end for the old Trent Dilfer. Not the beginning of a perfect person, as he still readily admits, but the beginning of real purpose in life for a rising star. The beginning of a new life that would better suit his needs as the next years of his athletic life would unfold.

That previous year of hypocrisy lay heavily on Dilfer's heart now. He knew, for instance, that he had played a lot of good people for the fool—especially Joe Broussard, the man who had endorsed Trent's Christian faith.

Joe was the man who had "discovered" Trent while he was on a visitation call from his church. Dilfer had assured Joe that he was a Christian, so when Broussard began working with FCA later that year, he figured Dilfer would be a great candidate to speak to young people.

"Now he regretted this," Dilfer says in retrospect. "But he didn't know what I was doing."

So, in the year after Dilfer got things straight with Jesus Christ, he went out on the road again—but this time as a changed man with a legitimate message, not as a hypocrite looking for more glory. "The neatest thing that God did was that after I was saved, He gave me so many opportunities to go back and erase the bad things I had done.

"He gave me a platform at Fresno that's unbelievable. I say this as humbly as I can, but I spoke to over 40,000 kids in a year and a half. I spoke to Rotary, Lion's Club, groups of men and women getting together. Every time I spoke, first I gave my testimony and I let them know what I had done in the past. Then I said, 'Hey, please forgive me.' If it was a group I had spoken to before, I asked forgiveness from the group. I had so many opportunities to just serve Christ those last few years I was in college."

During his party time at Fresno State, Dilfer had done all he could to impress people, but he had to end up apologizing to them. As a big football star and as an ace party animal, he had made his share of friends, but after trusting Jesus, he realized that they were not the kind of friends he needed. It was becoming clear that the Dilfer difference would mean a different set of friends.

"God blessed me with an unbelievable group of friends. Before that summer at the camp," he recalls, "I had not a single friend that I would call anything close to a Christian. God immediately threw three guys into my life who were stud Christians, who just took me under their wing and said, 'Hey, we're going to show you how to live a life for Christ.'"

And then there was the matter of students of the opposite sex. In his party days—or perhaps *daze* would describe it better—Dilfer showed little respect for young women. He was a love 'em and leave 'em kind of guy. "Then God put Cass into my life," Dilfer says, speaking of Cassandra, who is now his wife.

"Cass and I were friends when I was a freshman and sophomore, when I was messing around. She was a believer, and she didn't like the kind of person I was.

"We began a Bible study together. We learned together how to serve Christ, live for Him, and mold a relationship. We began as friends, but we saw the writing on the wall that we were eventually going to have a relationship, and God kind of drew a perfect picture for how our relationship was going to be. He took us both out of bad situations and put us into a good one."

So, in July of 1993, the summer before his junior year of football eligibility at Fresno, Trent Dilfer and Cassandra Franzman were married. The ceremony was performed by the man who had knocked on Dilfer's door two years earlier and had started him on the road to spiritual life—Joe Broussard.

With Trent's off-the-field life taken care of with his commitment to Jesus Christ and his relationship with Cass, the next order of business was to take advantage of his considerable football talents and see where they would take him.

The 1992 season had introduced Dilfer to the country as the leader of a high-powered offense. It was his first year as the sole owner of the quarterback slot for Fresno State, and he took full advantage of it. In an All-American year, Dilfer connected on 175 of 332 passes for 3,000 yards and 21 touchdowns. The Bulldogs ranked second in the nation in total offense and first in scoring, the kind of season that thrust Dilfer into the spotlight. The only blemish on this outstanding performance was Dilfer's problem with interceptions; he was picked off 14 times in his sophomore season.

Trent Dilfer, though, had already shown that he could change. He had done so when he shifted his allegiance from himself to Jesus Christ. He had done so when he retired from being a playboy and married Cass.

But could he change his quarterbacking style enough to eliminate the interceptions? And if he could, how far would his talents take him?

Expectations ran high in Fresno as the 1993 football campaign began. Besides Dilfer, the Bulldogs returned outstanding tailback Ron Rivers and Dilfer's favorite target, Malcolm Seabron, from a team that in 1992 had capped a successful season with a Freedom Bowl win over Southern Cal. Some preseason polls had Fresno State in the Top Ten.

And for Dilfer, the pressure was really on. For example, the Fresno State sports information department put together a press release titled "A Quarterback from FSU Should Win the Heisman." Of course most observers would read that to mean Florida State University QB Charlie Ward, not Fresno's Dilfer. But the comparison on the press release favored the young man from California.

He had Ward beat in numerous categories, including NCAA pass efficiency, total offense, passing yards, passing yards per game, touchdown passes, and games with at least three touchdown passes. But the statistic that most clearly showed the improvement for Dilfer—if not his right to have the Heisman—was in the area of interceptions.

Whereas he had tossed 14 passes to guys in the wrong-colored jerseys as a sophomore, in his junior year, Dilfer set an NCAA record by throwing 271 consecutive passes without an interception. For the year, he fired 333 passes and was picked but 4 times. His touchdown to interception ratio was an incredible 7 to 1.

But the 1993 Heisman Trophy was simply not meant to find its way into Trent and Cass's trophy case. Ward, of course, won the award, while Dilfer finished ninth in the balloting.

Brushing the disappointment aside, Dilfer was able to look at that situation with maturity. "I think Charlie Ward is just the greatest," Dilfer said after the other FSU quarterback won the Heisman. "I think he's the best player in college football this year, and I think he's a great person. I don't think it could happen to a nicer person. You know the thing you've got to look at is my numbers and some other quarterbacks' numbers may be better than Charlie's or some of the others—the Heath Shulers and so forth—but we're not playing Miami each week. And you know teams like that have great secondaries and great defensive lines. It's easier for us to put up big numbers. He's doing it where the game is at a different speed."

Charlie Ward would take his athletic skills to a sport noted for a much different speed—the fast-breaking, slam-dunking, quick-or-your're-dead NBA. But Dilfer was also to find out about moving his game up several notches.

After his junior year, Dilfer decided to skip his final year of eligibility in college and enter the NFL draft—the same draft that would leave Ward high and dry and headed for the hardwood.

For Dilfer though, the NFL future looked bright. His 6 feet 5, 230-pound body and his accurate throwing arm were just the attributes NFL scouts were salivating over. Heisman or no Heisman, Trent Dilfer was a hot draft topic, and the Tampa Bay Buccaneers quickly claimed him as booty, the sixth player taken in the draft.

Of his selection by Tampa Bay, Trent Dilfer said at the time that he "couldn't be happier about it." He and Cass were pictured in *Sports*

Illustrated, all smiles as they donned the Tampa Bay orange.

Can anything be more glorious for a twenty-two-year-old young man, with a beautiful wife, strong spiritual base, and a bright future in the National Football League?

Yet trouble was on the horizon. Quicker than you can say *training camp,* the gloss came off the shiny portrait of a young football star.

A camp had changed Dilfer's life just a few years earlier, but he was AWOL from this camp when he needed to be learning the ropes as an NFL quarterback. Dilfer was back home in Fresno during the twelve days of the Buccaneers' summer camp, having trouble with his new contract. When agreement finally came, Dilfer had signed an eight-year, multi million-dollar deal, but he also had given returning quarterback Craig Erickson a head start and had some "twelve days of catching up to do."

Here he was, a rich young Buc. *All I have to do is learn the playbook,* he figured. But as Dilfer later found out, the biggest problem in his life was not learning the playbook. It was learning how to deal with being young and rich and famous.

"I struggled very bad spiritually," he says, describing his first year in the NFL. "Both my wife and I struggled. This was a big chunk to chew off, being a rookie and having all that money. We learned the hard way.

"When you drift away from serving Christ," Dilfer says, "you start serving yourself. I think I was overwhelmed by the world and this whole NFL thing. I didn't have Christ as the center of my life. I kind of said, 'OK, God. You got me here. Now let me take over.'" It wasn't a situation in which he reverted back to his old ways of college. Instead, Dilfer says his wife and he struggled to maintain their relationship with Christ and each other.

To add to his troubles, the rich rookie was not doing much to earn his money on the field. He played in just five games for Tampa Bay, starting two of them.

Included in those starts is a game Dilfer still calls his highlight of his still young NFL career. "My first start was at Candlestick Park in front of a thousand friends and family against the eventual champion 49ers. Nobody can take that away from me. I played awful. The team played awful, but down the line I can say my very first start was against Deion Sanders—the greatest cornerback to ever play. And he didn't pick me off."

Finally and mercifully that first season was over. And so, in effect, was the Dilfers' spiritual funk. "Thank goodness for God's grace and His forgiveness and being able to come to Him and say, 'I blew it. Pull me back in.'"

The Dilfers used a conference at the end of the 1994 season to help pull them back in. It was the Professional Athletes Outreach conference, an opportunity headed by Norm Evans, a longtime Miami Dolphin.

At the football PAO, Trent and Cass rediscovered the importance of putting Christ first. "It was an opportunity for us to realize what the purpose of our life was, and that was to serve Christ and not be so caught up in the NFL and the money and the fame. It was to take the gifts that God has given, and use them to expand His kingdom—and not necessarily expand your ego. Since that time, we've really tried to strengthen our commitment and serve Christ in a much broader arena."

The 1995 season started much better for both Dilfer and the Bucs. During the off-season, he had worked almost daily with quarterbacks coach Turk Schonert, attempting to work the kinks out of his game. Early on in the season, the hard work paid off in a temporary first-place run by the Buccaneers. After six games, Tampa Bay stood atop the NFC Central Division.

After eight games, the Bucs were 6–2, and it looked like the losingest franchise in the past ten years was ready to assert itself as a contender for the division title. Capping off that first-half success was a home game against Minnesota. In what Dilfer calls "my best game as a professional," Tampa Bay defeated the Vikings' 20–17 in overtime.

He didn't know it at the time, but it may have been an important game for the future as he performed well in front of Tony Dungy, then the Vikings defensive coordinator, and later to become the Tampa Bay head coach.

What started out to be a breakthrough year for Tampa Bay soured after that Viking win. Seven losses in the next nine games cost Sam Wyche his job and opened the coaching door for Dungy.

Dungy saw Dilfer at his best on October 15, but he also saw him react to the frustration of a lost season about six weeks later. With the

Vikings leading 28–7 in a game at the Metrodome, Dilfer grew tired of the beating he was taking at the hands of the Vikes' defense. He had been sacked six times, so after defensive tackle John Randle tackled him hard after Dilfer had thrown an incompletion, the quarterback went after Randle and punched him. Dilfer was ejected. He had learned still another lesson as a student learning to be a top NFL quarterback.

It's an area he knows he needs to work on. "One of the things I struggle with in this league is the amount of time I'm on camera. I don't ever want to hurt God's credibility and His witness."

Still growing, still learning. Still making mistakes and owning up to them. Just like most Christians, Trent Dilfer is a Christian in process. The Bucs' chaplain, Doug Gilcrease, says of Trent, "He's growing and learning. He wants to serve the Lord."

It's not been a straight road to success for Trent Dilfer. Instead, he's gone up and down the bumpy hills and valleys of a football career filled with success and promise. Along the way he's taken spiritual detours, yet he always seems to get back on the right road.

He's a lot like all of us. We don't have his money or his fame. But we have similar struggles. We fight similar battles. And we can have the same resources. We might call it the Dilfer difference—the difference God makes in your life when you let Him be in charge. "Living the Christian life gives you joy and peace and love," Dilfer says. "It's such a wonderful gift to love people like you can when you're a Christian."

Q & A WITH TRENT DILFER

Q: *Do you have a biblical hero?*
Trent: Barnabas is kind of a biblical hero of mine. Recently, I was going through a frustrating stage of my knowledge of the Bible. I don't have the knowledge of the Bible I'd like to have. I was talking with one of my buddies, and he said, "You affect people's lives in so many different areas. Your gift isn't necessarily getting up and preaching and speaking, although you're good at it. God has provided for you in other areas." So when I get down on myself for not doing enough speaking or actual service out in the public, I get encouraged by knowing that through the people I'm helping, my friends and so forth, a lot of people are coming to know Christ. That's like Barnabas.

Q: *What legacy do you want to leave as an NFL player?*
Trent: As a player all I want them to say down the line, and it is early to ask this, is that he's a winner. I don't care about the stats. All-Pro and those things would be nice, but I just want to get better and win football games. I think the greatest compliment you can be given when you're finished is that "he won football games."

Q: *Do you have favorite Bible passage?*
Trent: Colossians 3:17: "And whatever you do, whether in word or deed, do it all in the name of the Lord Jesus Christ, giving thanks to God the Father through Him."

Q: *How do you and Cassandra keep sharp spiritually?*
Trent: We are involved in two major Bible studies. One with my team-mates on Monday night and then Thursday nights we have a Sunday school class that meets in our home. The women meet downstairs and the men upstairs. We do that for two and one-half hours on Thursday. In the off-season, we're involved with our Sunday school class. Cass is also involved with Bible Study Fellowship and a wives' study. She's involved in four Bible studies. She's really taken off. I'm doing a hermeneutics study with Doug Gilcrease, our Athletes in Action representative. I'm really digging into God's Word and getting a better understanding of it.

Jason Hanson
The Plug-in Kicker

VITAL STATISTICS

Born June 17, 1970 in Spokane, Washington
6 feet, 183 pounds
College: Washington State
Position: Kicker
1996 team: Detroit Lions

CAREER HIGHLIGHTS

- Led NFC in scoring with 130 points (1993)
- Connected on three game-winning kicks (1994)
- Voted to All-Rookie team in first NFL season. Was 30 for 30 on extra points
- Voted Offensive Rookie of the Year by *Pro Football Weekly*
- Selected college All-American kicker (1990, 1991)
- Kicked longest field goal in NCAA history without a tee, 62 yards
- Holds NCAA records for most field goals of 50 yards or longer (20) and most field goals of 40 yards or longer (39)

WARMING UP

In his first game out of the blocks, against Mike Ditka's Chicago Bears, Hanson nailed his only field goal attempt, a 38-yarder, and all three point-after attempts. The Bears won the game, though, when Jim Harbaugh led a scoring drive that ended in a TD pass to Tom Waddle as time expired to lift the Monsters of the Midway past the gang from Motown, 27–24. There would be no late-game heroics this September afternoon for Hanson, but he served notice that he belonged.

Hanson went on to put together an outstanding rookie season: 30 for 30 point after touchdowns (PATs), a string of twelve straight successful field goals, and an 80.8 percent completion rate on field goals. Hanson was named by *Pro Football Weekly* as the Offensive Rookie of the Year, and he was also named to several All-Rookie teams.

Jason Hanson

Detroit, Michigan. Season opener in 1994. Overtime with the score Atlanta 28, Detroit 28. Enter Jason Hanson of the Lions, who calmly puts his foot into the football and nails a 37-yard field goal for the win.

Irving, Texas. Two weeks later. Again it's overtime with Dallas and Detroit tied at 17. It's time for Jason Hanson, who strokes a 44-yard kick through the uprights as the Lions down the defending champion Cowboys.

East Rutherford, New Jersey. Five weeks later. Once again it's overtime with New York and Detroit tied at 25. Jason Hanson strolls onto the field and splits the uprights with a 24-yard game-winner.

Detroit, Michigan. September 25, 1995. It's the fourth quarter: San Francisco 24, Detroit 24. With less than two minutes left in the game, Jason Hanson steps before the ABC Monday Night Football cameras and drills a 32-yard field goal to defeat the defending champion San Francisco 49ers.

When the Detroit Lions plug in Jason Hanson with the game on the line, you can send the Goodyear blimp home. He has made a career of kicking his team to victory.

Along the route from his hometown of Spokane, Washington, to NFL stardom in the Motor City, Hanson has received some pretty good advice that has helped guide his powerful right foot. Included in that advice were two vital messages—one from a high school English teacher and one from a pastor in Pullman, Washington.

Those messages have been the centerpiece of Hanson's plug-in power both on the field and off.

To get to the point where either bit of advice would do him any good, Hanson first carved out for himself a rather impressive record as a kid.

In athletics, he and his brother Travis established themselves early on as something special. They spent much of their free time sending soccer balls flying all over the neighborhood. It was clear that Jason, especially, was a born soccer player.

"I was a soccer player all my life, thinking I was going to be the next Pelé," he confesses. "I think soccer is a great team sport. It reminds me slightly of chess, because it has a lot of strategy. It's a lot of movement, a lot of self-control."

Beginning at age six, young Jason played soccer year-round. "I'd get a little basketball in the winter, but football season interfered with soccer and baseball season interfered with soccer. It was so much fun, and it was so competitive and exciting. I had dreams of being the best. I thought, *That's all I'm gonna do is play soccer.*"

Fortunately for the Detroit Lions, the Washington State Cougars, and even for Jason Hanson, that's not all he ended up doing. Because soccer was a spring sport in the Pacific Northwest, Hanson's autumns were freed up enough to allow him to dabble in the sport that features the ball with points at both ends.

"Soccer was my first love," he explains, "but I realized that it was hard to get a college scholarship, and past that level there wasn't any league at all. With the option there to play football and get a scholarship as a kicker, I decided that was the smart way to go."

As a sophomore at Mead High School in Spokane, he played JV football. As a junior, his star rose so quickly that he became an All-American punter. Soon the college recruiters were at his door.

When they saw him kick during his senior year, they went away shaking their heads. Not because of booming kicks from midfield, but because he was having a lousy year. Having attracted the colleges in a stellar junior year, Hanson fell apart as a kicker during his senior year. He made just four of his twelve field goal attempts, effectively eliminating any chance of getting that college scholarship he had dreamed about earlier.

His was a nightmarish season, and Jason needed help. A wise, caring high school English teacher now entered the scene. Ron Chadwick, who doubled as an English teacher and football coach, pulled Jason aside during his senior year. It was about midseason, and Jason was struggling. "The kicks weren't going like I thought they should," Jason recalls.

"Do you make sure you have a routine that you do every time you kick?" Chadwick asked. "You need to do the same thing every time."

As Hanson says, "He brought up some ideas about consistency and habits . . . that up to that point I had never really thought about. All I knew was that I kicked the ball. He was really the first person who made me think, *I've got to develop an exact routine.* That got me on track to think about what it takes to be an accurate field goal kicker.

"It was almost just in passing. I began to think, *Maybe he's right.*"

No maybe about it. It revolutionized Hanson's kicking game. "Even today," Hanson explains, "it's the simple things that help you the most, even as a pro. You can get so analytical, but some of it is just focusing on those little things. Now, instead of thinking, *There's 8 seconds left and I've got to win the game,* I just do what I know how to do."

But to get to where he is today, he first had to get to college. Four-of-twelve field goal kicking as a senior meant football was not his ticket into a major college. But he did have something more valuable than a perfect kicking percentage. He had a perfect grade point average.

"I did well," Hanson says quietly about his high school classroom days. "I enjoyed my school and my teachers. I was a 4.0 [GPA] student. School was always important to me. I tried to work as hard in the classroom as I did at sports."

So, off to Pullman, Washington, went this 6-foot, 180-pound, good-looking, athletic kid, accompanied by his perfect grade point average and his desire to become a doctor. Soccer was behind him now, and perhaps so was football. Like so many other high school jocks, his days of basketball, football, and soccer seemed destined to become memories to be recalled, not new heroics to be experienced.

Yet Jason Hanson was not about to give up. He decided to try out for the team as a walk-on at Washington State. He showed up at practice, equipped with his powerful leg and with Ron Chadwick's advice still fresh on his mind.

But this would be no story of Rudy, the walk-on who had four years of practice for Notre Dame and one cameo appearance on the field. In the kind of scene that itself would make a good movie script, Hanson was awarded a WSU uniform from Cougar coach Dennis Erickson after he saw the youngster boot long-distance field goals with either foot. "He is the best kicker I've ever seen," Erickson concluded.

And he would become, by many accounts, the best college kicker anyone had ever seen.

From his first successful varsity try—a 41-yarder against Illinois—to his final field goal for the Cougars, Jason Hanson combined his somewhat unorthodox style with his newfound ability to concentrate on keeping the routine the same each time. The result was a remarkable college career.

Most remarkable was what happened on September 28, 1991. Washington State was playing the University of Nevada at Las Vegas, and Hanson was called on to attempt a long-distance field goal of 62 yards. No college football player had accomplished such a . . . well, *feat*, . . . since kicking tees had been outlawed in 1988.

For further comparison, consider that the NFL record, held by Tom Dempsey, is just one yard longer. And that record had stood for more than two decades.

Characteristically, Hanson was successful on this kick, thus cementing his place in college football history. Hanson became the first college kicker using a human holder to connect from that distance.

Two years earlier he captured national attention in a game televised on ESPN. WSU won against Brigham Young, but Hanson stole the show with field goals of 46, 52, and 58 yards. "It was on national television," Hanson remembers, "and it was the first game where I proved that I could kick the long ones. I guess I kind of broke through. Up to that point I had confidence and I knew I could kick, but I never pondered anything about national attention and what it meant. After the game there was just a buzz, and I realized that it was a big deal. It was the first time I had experienced this. It stuck in my mind."

While Washington State was learning the secret to plugging in Jason Hanson for challenging scoring situations and watching the electricity happen, the young man with the legacy-making leg was learning about another kind of being plugged in. His education would come as he received that second message, the one from the Pullman pastor.

To understand the power of that message, we need to return to

Hanson's soccer days, back when he was, as he describes, "just your typical kid who tried to play sick on Sundays." Back then, "Sunday school was fine, but I couldn't stand to have to sit through church," he admits.

"But there came a point when I was ten or eleven when it was made clear to me that just because I went to church or just because my parents were Christians did not mean I was going to heaven." It was a point when he knew he had to make a decision about Jesus Christ.

"I decided that, 'Hey, this is true. I want to accept Christ. I want to be forgiven.' So I accepted Christ."

We aren't talking about a dramatic turnaround here. No "I was on drugs and came to the end of my life" story here. Just a kid who realized that he was a sinner who needed a Savior.

"Going through junior high and high school, I was a good kid," Jason explains. "I didn't dabble in the drugs and the drinking. It's great that I don't have to look back with regret. Or have any consequences now that I'm dealing with for any foolish decisions that I would have made then. I was definitely a good kid who loved God and knew my faith was real."

Yet as happens so often with teenagers—even good ones in great homes—there wasn't much spiritual growth in high school. Never in any trouble, but also never overly fired up about his faith.

That began to change, though, when as a deeper-thinking college student Hanson saw life with a new perspective. It was a perspective that would call on him to make some important commitments.

"Through success in football at college," he says, "I began to think about all the accolades I got in college—all the incredible things like being All-American. It occurred to me one day that if this is all life has to offer, 'Whoa! We're in big trouble.'

"I was getting everything any football player needed, but when I went back to college after a road trip, my homework was still waiting for me. Life was still there. The problems that I had before I left were still there. Football really only changed my point of view for a weekend, and then when I went back, it all came back.

"Now, I had accepted Christ, but I began to realize what life would be without Him. I began to realize that if I didn't have Christ, there would be a hole in my heart that this isn't filling."

In a sense, Hanson was trying to conquer college life and keep his football career in balance as a Lone Ranger. That's why he needed the insightful question posed to him by a pastor of a church he attended occasionally in Pullman. The pastor, Neal Swanson, approached the football player one day and asked, "Jason, are you plugged in down here?"

Pastor Swanson had the second message for Hanson, and it came in the form of two questions.

"Do you have a spiritual outlet down here [in Pullman]? And do you have people you can talk to and fellowship with and someone to disciple you?"

"Yeah, at home I have my church and all my friends," Hanson answered. Included among that group was his girlfriend, Kathleen McCloskey. He lived only an hour away from Spokane, so it was easy to go home on the weekends.

But that answer didn't satisfy Pastor Swanson.

"He really wanted to meet with me once a week to make sure I was being fed," Hanson says. "Kind of discipling me."

Despite his original reluctance, Hanson agreed, and has been thankful about it ever since. He benefited by being plugged in. "That was really a blessing. It was something God had in store for me. Neal wanted to make sure I had somebody here to talk to about spiritual things. That was something that God used to disciple me and help me mature."

The concept of being plugged in spiritually has continued to follow Hanson through the years.

And now he shares that principle with Kathleen, whom he married in 1992. Ironically, though they went to the same elementary school, the same junior high, the same high school, and the same church, "We didn't really meet until college," Jason says.

When Jason went away to school in Pullman, Kathleen stayed in Spokane and attended Whitworth College. On those weekends home from WSU, Jason would get together with church friends and "goof around," as he describes it.

"All of a sudden I was meeting and goofing around with older kids. Sure enough, Kathy was one of them."

Their marriage was the third highlight for Jason Hanson in a memorable 1992. First, he was drafted by the Detroit Lions in the second round. The Lions were so impressed with Hanson that they let their all-time leading field goal kicker, Eddie Murray, move on. The job was Hanson's.

Second, Hanson graduated from Washington State, with a glossy 3.8 grade point average in pre-med studies. He was named a WSU Presidential Scholar recipient and a member of the GTE/CoSIDA Academic All-American team.

Third, in the summer preceding his rookie year in the NFL, Jason and Kathleen were married.

Then it was time for some football.

It was a grand brand of football the rookie played for the Lions. In his first game out of the blocks, against Mike Ditka's Chicago Bears, Hanson nailed his only field goal attempt, a 38-yarder, and all three point-after attempts. The Bears won the game, though, when Jim Harbaugh led a scoring drive that ended in a TD pass to Tom Waddle as time expired to lift the Monsters of the Midway past the gang from Motown, 27–24. There would be no late-game heroics this September afternoon for Hanson, but he served notice that he belonged.

At first, Hanson wasn't convinced it would be easy to feel like he belonged in an NFL locker room. Although he had been very well accepted at Washington State as a little guy among the behemoths, he knew things would be different for him in the pros.

"Being a rookie and coming in as a kicker is kind of two strikes against you," he says of the normal rookie status. But Hanson knew how to defuse any problems. First, he did it with his demeanor. "The key is to just treat everybody with respect. I just try to get along with everybody." Second, he did it with his foot, which was his major goal. "My main goal is not to play like a rookie," he said during his initial year. "I want to step out and be like a seasoned veteran NFL kicker and handle the pressure."

Scoring six points against the Bears in front of a big Soldier Field crowd proved that he was up to the task. Hanson went on to put together an outstanding rookie season: 30 for 30 point after touchdowns (PATs), a string of twelve straight successful field goals, and an 80.8 percent completion rate on field goals. Hanson was named by *Pro Football Weekly* as the Offensive Rookie of the Year, and he was also named to several All-Rookie teams.

As the years have gone by and Hanson has continued to improve, he's learned to face the temptations and pitfalls that come to many professional athletes. He's learned not to be "consumed by the pressures of football," as he puts it.

One of the pressures, surprisingly enough, is money. In a league that has opened its purse strings in a big-time way, there seems to be little happiness about the subject. Hanson understands the problem.

He faced it after the 1994 season when the Lions named him a transitional player. This meant that he was a free agent, open to look at offers from any other team. The Lions would then have the right to match any such offer. It could have been a time for Hanson to play one side against the other and laugh about it all the way to the bank.

"I'm not really concerned about moving to the next spot," he said at the time. "It's all big money anyway. A lot of guys want the bigger contract, but it's just a matter of pride. It's almost an I'm-better-than-you kind of thing. I found myself thinking about that as I watched other kickers sign for big money. But really, money's got nothing to do with it. I need to just worry about sticking the ball through the uprights."

Hanson has captured a spirit that is all too rare in pro sports. "People think, *If you have money, you'll be happy.* We have a life that we could never dream of. We don't have to worry about the temporary things, like paying the bills. We are blessed beyond comprehension.

"I find that God is teaching us the very same things you learn if you don't have money. Whether you are rich or poor, the same lessons, the same discipling, the same shaping by God takes place. I hope I'm humble and I hope the money's not important. Yet, when there's lots of it, it's so easy to lose perspective.

"We share the same disappointments as people who aren't earning the money we earn in pro football. We do have nice things, but it hit me not long ago—it's going to be gone soon. If my hope was in money, then as soon as I'm done with football, then what?"

Yes, you read those words right. A pro athlete who seems to have the money monster under control. Refreshing, isn't it? But not surprising. Not when you consider what Hanson and his wife do to keep that perspective on target. And not when you remember what Hanson learned from Pastor Swanson.

"When we came to Detroit, we searched for someplace to get plugged in, to find a church. And God provided. When we first came here, we weren't sure if we were going to stay here or if we were going to move back home. But we knew that if we were here between six months to a year, we had to find a church. We found a good church here for us. I remembered what I had learned back in Pullman. Just because I had Christian friends back home and because my parents still go to the same church, that doesn't count for me or for Kathy."

The Hansons also got involved in the spiritual goings-on with the Lions. Led by chaplain Dave Wilson, they are involved with team Bible studies, and Kathleen is active in women's Bible studies that she and some of the other wives attend.

"That plugged-in concept is vital," Jason reiterates. "We knew we needed to meet other Christians and be into the Word. So we got plugged in right away. The fastest way to start drowning spiritually is not to do that—not to get plugged in. You can have your Bible studies and your prayer time, and that's certainly key, but I also believe that God wants us to be in a place of fellowship and accountable to other people who worship Him.

"I think that any time we haven't been fellowshiping—we've been too much out of touch with other Christians and too much into football—we've struggled. I think that's how God intended it. We were never supposed to be out there on our own, [as] renegade Christians."

On the field, there was one time period in the 1994 season during which he somehow came unplugged. Reminiscent of his tough senior year in high school, Hanson struggled to master the kicking game.

"Just when you think you've got it figured out," Hanson muses, "things go sour." Although he set an NFL record with three game-winning kicks in overtime that year, his field-goal percentage was an un-Hansonlike 66 percent (18 of 27). Against Tampa Bay his troubles were most apparent, as he missed his first-ever kick from inside 42 yards. He had nailed 44 straight from that distance or less in his pro career.

Part of the reason for the decline in his numbers during 1994 was a shin injury he suffered making a tackle against the Atlanta Falcons in game one of the season.

"That year was my biggest disappointment as a pro," Hanson says. Yet even in those tough days, the always optimistic Hanson found something to be positive about. "Even in my sourest moments in pro sports, I can look back and say it's made me a better football player. In my quest to be a better player, it helped me make changes I wouldn't normally have changed."

Watch Jason Hanson the next time you see the Lions play. See if he doesn't follow the good advice of his high school coach. See if he doesn't calmly follow the same routine each time he approaches a kick. Whether it's the first quarter with no score or in overtime with 72,000 Silverdome fans screaming for him to deliver, he approaches the kick the same way.

It's all part of the secret of being plugged in.

Q & A WITH JASON HANSON

Q: *What is your favorite ministry opportunity?*
Jason: Working with kids. I love kids. I love to play with little kids. I love to talk to high school and college age young adults. That's an age group I love to share my testimony with.

Q: *What would be a theme for a typical Jason Hanson talk?*
Jason: One theme I talk about comes from 1 Timothy 4:8. "Bodily discipline is only of little profit, but godliness is profitable for all things" (NASB). I tell them that as a pro athlete, I have to take my eyes off the temporary—off the cars, the wealth, the fame—and get my eyes on Christ and God. I tell them that you look at pro athletes and it seems that they have everything, but really, we have nothing unless we have Christ.

Q: *What is your favorite Bible passage?*
Jason: James 1:17, "Every good and perfect gift is from above, coming down from the Father of the heavenly lights, who does not change like shifting shadows."

Q: *What is your biggest interest outside of football, family, and faith?*
Jason: Music. I played the trumpet in junior high and really liked music, but there was a point in high school where music was like a sport, and it took the same dedication that the sports took, and I couldn't divide my time. So I chose to pursue sports. But to this day, music is my favorite interest—outside of football.

Now, as a professional athlete and having a better sense of what it takes to have a mastery of a skill, I look at the great musicians and marvel. I think it's such an awesome gift and talent.

I haven't picked up my trumpet in a long time. The chaplain here on the team is trying to get me to learn the guitar. I might take it up. My wife has a piano, and she can play it pretty well.

I really like Steven Curtis Chapman. He did a chapel in Detroit for the Lions. That was really funny because we were all gawking and acting like kids before he came, and the chaplain said, "You guys are acting like the fans that you joke about." So we felt kind of embarrassed. Nobody combines lyrics and melodies as well as SCC.

Q: *What do you like to do for leisure activities?*
Jason: The whole outdoor thing. My wife loves to hike. On our honeymoon we went to Banff, Canada. I think the mountains and that kind of thing excite us. My wife gets into the beach, but I think together we prefer the outdoors and hiking.

Chad Hennings
Man on a Mission

VITAL STATISTICS

Born October 20, 1965 in Elberon, Iowa
6 feet 6, 288 pounds
College: Air Force
Position: Defensive Tackle
1996 team: Dallas Cowboys

CAREER HIGHLIGHTS

- Played on three Super Bowl championship teams (1993, 1994, 1996)
- Sacked quarterbacks 7.5 times in 1994
- 1987 Outland Trophy winner and college All-American
- Set Western Athletic Conference record with 24 sacks (1987)

WARMING UP

I magine having these things offered to you and not being able to grab them: a huge NFL contract, pro football fame, and the chance to play for the legendary Cowboys. Wouldn't we be tempted to say to him, "Boy, Chad, too bad about the mistake. Too bad you didn't know what you were doing when you reenlisted after your sophomore year. Goodness, you could have transferred back home to Iowa, harassed Big Ten quarterbacks for two years, and then backed up the truck to the NFL Bounty Bank."

To which Hennings would reply, "It was no mistake at all. It all goes back to what my dad and mom said, 'Once you start something, you never quit.' So, it wasn't an option. Sure it was tough to swallow, but I committed myself to this, and I was going to stick to it.

"My natural agenda would have been to go into professional football right out of college," Hennings says, "but God had other plans for me. I had to mature physically, emotionally, and spiritually before I was ever ready to hit the NFL. God molded me."

Chad Hennings

I f you're up on Super Bowl history, you probably remember some scenes from the 1996 Super Bowl. Scenes like Pittsburgh quarterback Neil O'Donnell firing strikes to Dallas cornerback Larry Brown, who grabbed those two passes for interceptions to seal the Cowboys' victory and earn himself a piece of football history as the game MVP.

But if you're really up on the Super Bowl—if you pay attention to players whose uniforms don't have numbers below thirty and whose names aren't Troy Aikman and Emmitt Smith, you'll recall the name Chad Hennings from Super Bowl XXX. And you'll recall that big number 95 had an important role in causing one of those errant passes that ended up hitting Brown in the numbers.

For Hennings, it was almost as big a game as a defensive tackle will get. A defensive player can't rack up too many glamour statistics, and he is paid mostly for sacrificing his body in an effort to get to the quarterback or the running back. He gets his due by playing a solid supporting role.

In Super Bowl XXX, Hennings supported the Cowboys in a huge way. The huge tackle recorded two quarterback sacks and three tackles. Hennings was on a mission—and he accomplished it well.

If you're up on Super Bowl history, you know that. And if you're also up on your recent American history, you probably recall some scenes from the 1991 Persian Gulf War: accurate missiles finding their targets in a 100-hour war, and at war's end the burning oil fields of Kuwait and pictures of the Kurdish people fleeing their homes—rushing into the mountains to escape the onslaught of the Iraqis. Fearful of their lives, the Kurds left everything. Without provisions, shelter, or even clear direction, they ran in desperation.

During the exodus, the United States and other coalition countries sought to provide assistance for those people. Risking their lives as they flew across enemy territory, young coalition pilots carried vital provisions northward and parachuted them down to the Kurds.

One scene you may not recall was of a future NFL star, Chad Hennings, providing aerial support. Flying an A-10 Tankbuster, also known as a Warthog, pilot Hennings spent several months on a mission of mercy, helping to make sure the Kurds were not overrun. He and his Air Force buddies flew more than four hours across southern Turkey into northern Iraq.

"At first, we were escorting relief drops to the Kurds," Hennings recalls. But as the relief mission was winding down, Hennings's assignment changed. "After they got the Kurds back down out of the mountains, our mission became one of reconnaissance. Basically, we were making sure the Iraqis were doing what they were supposed to be doing according to the peace agreement they had signed. They weren't supposed to fly in the no-fly zone. And we were making sure they weren't starting any more buildups in the north."

Battling Leon Searcy and the Pittsburgh Steelers may seem a fearsome task, but it surely doesn't compare with flying a Warthog across unfriendly territory. For Hennings, the danger of being shot down was real, yet he contends that the likelihood of that happening was small.

"They did have stuff to shoot at us," he reports, "and we flew over some surface-to-air missile sites as well as some anti-aircraft gun batteries, but they never fired on us. They were stupid if they did, because they would just get decimated. They weren't stupid people. They learned their lesson quick. They did have some firepower, but they didn't have the firepower to sustain it."

Chad Hennings doesn't speak of battling enemies such as the Steelers and the Iraqis with any special excitement or sense of wonder. Instead, he speaks with a firm intensity, perhaps as a NASA engineer would describe the critical moments of a Space Shuttle liftoff or the way a noted surgeon would describe a delicate transplant procedure. No glitz, no drummed-up thrills. Just the facts—facts that need no dressing up, for they have their own drama.

For Hennings, that kind of firm confidence comes from a life in which he has taken on mission after mission with success—which is just what would be expected from the product of an Iowa farm where hard work was the norm and the dreams were as big as the summer sky above the cornfields.

The Hennings farm is a nine-hundred-acre spread near the tiny eastern Iowa village of Elberon. There the family worked together to grow corn and soybeans and raise upwards of 2,500 head of cattle.

And there the Hennings boys learned the value of hard work and sticking to a task. Put another way, that's where they learned to face each new chore as a mission that had to be completed.

"My parents taught me that once you start something, be committed to it 100 percent until it's completed. 'If you want to be successful,' they would say, 'you're going to have to work at it. You're going to have to put in the extra time and do the little things right.'"

Hennings found out how serious his parents were about that after he expressed a desire to take guitar lessons. When he asked his dad about it, Chad was told, "Fine, but you're going to follow through with it."

It wasn't long before Chad had had enough of the guitar. "I didn't anticipate having to sit down for a half hour to forty-five minutes every day to practice. I wanted to be outside playing."

But he had made a commitment, and his parents thought he should keep it. "From that point on, they said, 'You started it, it's something you committed yourself to, now finish it.' I took guitar all the way through elementary school, sports programs, school work, everything, up through junior high. It was something that was instilled in me at a young age."

Along the way, Hennings began other pursuits that helped him learn the importance of sticking to a task. For instance, he was involved with 4-H, a group that helps train kids who want to learn more about agriculture. In this adventure, Hennings raised calves. "I learned what it takes to start with a young calf, learn to feed it, halterbreak it, and care for it. It was like training that calf, almost like an athlete, to go perform at a fair."

He also found time for sports, initially baseball and wrestling. "I attended wrestling tournaments since I was in third grade," he says. "In Iowa, everyone wrestles. You're born with a singlet on and headgear."

Well, maybe not quite, but it was certainly one sport that Hennings could carry through with, just as he had been taught to do. In fact, he was so successful at grappling he became a state champion wrestler at Benton Community High School.

But if there was one sport that Chad faced with a continuing sense of mission, it was football. "Every little kid in America dreams of playing in the NFL," Hennings says. "My goal was that I always wanted to be an All-American football player."

It didn't hurt that he was, as he calls himself, "the mutant of the family. I'm 6 feet 6 and weigh 290. My brother is 6' and weighs 225." So, besides being a state champion wrestler, Hennings earned spots on the Iowa All-State football team in both his junior and senior years at Benton.

Despite his 4-H activities and his sports success, he kept his balance, serving on the student council, earning National Honor Society recognition for his academics, and being active at church. He was so well balanced that when it came time to decide what college to attend, he had an opportunity many young people covet but never achieve. He won an appointment to the Air Force Academy in Colorado Springs.

A more natural place to attend college might have been Iowa. After all, the Iowa Hawkeyes were the family favorite. And they did try to recruit Chad—as did Iowa State, Purdue, and Minnesota.

But Hennings wasn't interested in making the easy choice. "I wanted to go out of state. I wanted to travel and see the world. I was always intrigued by the military and that lifestyle. I wanted the challenge, but first I wanted the education."

Sounds a bit like a mission, don't you think?

"I wasn't sure what I wanted to major in, but with the Air Force Academy's curriculum, you get a taste of everything. It's a well-rounded, balanced education." In the end, Hennings majored in management at the Air Force Academy.

And he also was able to live out his dream of playing college football. It wasn't easy, but it was possible because of what he had learned from his parents about staying on task. At the Air Force Academy, football players are treated no different from anyone else. "Even if you play football, you're expected to do everything else—all your military training, your whole academic program. And we had to make our bed, march to lunch, and do all that other stuff."

"All that other stuff" included an episode that Hennings thinks of as one of his highlights at the Air Force: Survival training. As soon as his freshman year was over, Hennings and his classmates headed for the hills. They were taken into the Rocky Mountains, where they spent a couple of weeks existing as escaped prisoners of war or downed pilots. The mission in this case was to survive unharmed, which seems to be great training for both football players and pilots.

And, of course, as his mission in Operation Provide Comfort in Iraq would indicate, Hennings also began his pilot training while at the Academy. It wasn't exactly a big dream of his to become a pilot, but when he got the chance, he took advantage of it. "We had summer programs. I'd go fly in a glider and in single engine Cessnas." It was a far cry from an A-10 Thunderbolt, but it got his flying career off the ground.

In between the marching, the studying, the surviving, and the flying, Hennings had time for football.

Hennings may have been fulfilling his dream by playing college football, and he may think that every kid in America dreams of playing in the NFL, but Hennings did not really think he had a chance at the big time during his four years with the Falcons. "The professional aspect—thinking that I had a shot at the NFL," he says, "never really entered my mind until I started getting selected to All-American teams after my senior year."

As he prepared for his last year at the academy, Hennings and his teammates knew they had a tough road ahead. Nine of the eleven defensive starters from the 1986 team had graduated. So it was up to Hennings to set the pace for the defense.

In the team's first game of 1987, he did just that. Against Wyoming, Hennings had seven tackles, three quarterback sacks, one fumble recovery, and three batted passes. Behind Hennings' defense and the quarterbacking of Dee Dowis, Air Force surprised the experts by starting strong and playing well enough to face Arizona State in a post-season bowl game.

Another typical outing for Hennings in his senior year was the Falcons' eighth game, against the University of Texas-El Paso, who was 5–1 going into the game. Before the game, UTEP coach Bob Stull told his charges that they had to do two things: control Chad Hennings and Dee Dowis. After the game, he concluded, "We did neither one."

All Hennings did was sack UTEP QB Pat Hegarty three times, create another tackle for a loss, and frustrate UTEP linemen into four holding penalties as they tried to contain him. The Falcons whipped the Miners 35–7.

For the year, Hennings set a Western Athletic Conference record with 24 sacks and was named the WAC Defensive Player of the Year. In addition, he was named an All-American and won the Outland Trophy as the best lineman in the land.

In a sense, for Chad Hennings, it was a mission accomplished. He had completed what he had started way back as a little kid when he and his brother first went at it in football. He had made it to the top of his game in college. And so in April 1988, the Dallas Cowboys used an eleventh-round draft pick on Hennings, knowing full well that they couldn't sign him. At least not in that decade.

As they had done more than two decades earlier with Naval Academy graduate Roger Staubach, the Cowboys were willing to use one of their draft picks for a guy who still had several years of military commitment ahead of him.

Yes, there was another mission that Hennings still had to complete. When he signed up for his four-year hitch at the Air Force Academy, he also signed on for a post-academy assignment of up to eight years. If all went according to plan, he would not be eligible to suit up for the Cowboys until 1996.

Imagine having these things offered to you and not being able to grab them: a huge NFL contract, pro football fame, and the chance to play for the legendary Cowboys. Wouldn't we be tempted to say to him, "Boy, Chad, too bad about the mistake. Too bad you didn't know what you were doing when you reenlisted after your sophomore year. Goodness, you could have transferred back home to Iowa, harassed Big Ten quarterbacks for two years, and then backed up the truck to the NFL Bounty Bank."

To which Hennings would reply, "It was no mistake at all. It all goes back to what my dad and mom said, 'Once you start something, you never quit.' So, it wasn't an option. Sure it was tough to swallow, but I committed myself to this, and I was going to stick to it.

"My natural agenda would have been to go into professional football right out of college," Hennings says, "but God had other plans for me. I had to mature physically, emotionally, and spiritually before I was ever ready to hit the NFL. God molded me. . . . I grew a lot as a Christian because of my time in the military. It was all for a purpose."

In fact, Chad Hennings might conceivably not be the strong Christian he is today if he had charged right out of college and into a Cowboy training camp.

It was not as if Hennings had a foxhole conversion while in the military, though. He had grown up in the church, and was familiar with the Bible and Jesus Christ. "I had a very good foundation in the church I was brought up in," he says. "My church was really into studying the Bible. But I don't think I ever knew what it meant to experience a personal relationship with Jesus. Now I know I'm saved by the grace of God instead of by anything I've done.

"I became born again when I was in the military. I had a military chaplain who was very instrumental in my life. From there on, my faith has really been cultivated."

Hennings compares his spiritual training time to that of Moses' time in the desert. Happily, Hennings's backside-of-the-desert experience did not take forty years as Moses' did, or even the eight years that Chad thought it would. After serving in the Persian Gulf War and finishing that mission, Hennings continued to fulfill his military commitment; but then everything changed. In early 1992, the military began a major reduction in forces. "With all the government cutbacks in military spending," Hennings explained, "they wanted to cut down on pilots as well as other military personnel.

"They were waiving all kinds of our military commitments, but most important, they waived my pilot training commitment, which is eight years."

However, big Chad still had an Air Force Academy commitment of one year remaining. But then an official decided to waive it for the maturing football prospect. "It was something they had never done before," Hennings marvels. "So I was able to get out after four years of active duty."

For the first time since 1985, Hennings had an option. He had fulfilled his mission, and the military was telling him, "Hey, if you want out to do other things, go with our blessing."

It wasn't something that anyone could have predicted. Hennings puts it in historical perspective when he says that all it took to allow him to get out early was "for peace to break out all over the world."

And that could only happen, Hennings feels, because "The power of prayer is awesome." (Yes, he and his friends had been praying.)

Now it was time to test the power of Chad Hennings. Sure, he had won all those awards back in 1987, and sure, the Cowboys owned the rights to him. But after four years away from football, would he be in shape to battle the big boys in the NFL? And would he even remember how to do so?

His first workout under the watchful eye of Coach Jimmy Johnson and owner Jerry Jones in April 1992 seemed to indicate that he could. Perhaps Hennings didn't know it at the time, but the Double JJs had designs on trading Hennings for a middle-round draft pick. But when they saw the blond-headed Iowan up close and personal running through some timed drills, they quickly changed their minds.

Hennings had added twelve pounds to his college playing weight. But bigger didn't mean slower. First, he ran the 40-yard dash in 4.80— faster than every college senior defensive linemen but one in the NFL combine that spring. Then, when he ran through a pass-rush drill faster than some of the best young linebackers in the game, the Cowboys' brass knew they had a winner. Soon his name was on a contract, and he was headed to Big D.

As his workout for the Dallas head honchos had shown, Hennings had been working out while in the service. "I had lifted weights religiously," he says. "The Air Force encourages its pilots to lift weights in order to stand the G-forces and to have a good, strong cardiovascular system. So I lifted weights four or five days a week.

"But I hadn't put on the pads or a football helmet for four years." Which meant one thing. When he reported for training camp as a twenty-six-year-old rookie, Hennings had some making up to do. "It was an adjustment based on survival more than anything. I was just as strong as they were and as fast—speed wasn't a problem. It was just a matter of technique—getting back the moves that were just second nature to me, and to chip off the rust.

"It took quite a while. Training camp helped a lot, but you need the game experience. Once the season starts, I wasn't playing in any of the games. It was just practice, and you need the games to chip off that rust."

It took a while during his first year to see any game action. And that came mostly because of an unusual request. For the first five games of the 1992 season, Hennings was deactivated, which meant he was not eligible to play. Finally, on October 18, two days before his twenth-seventh birthday, he suited up for his very first NFL game. However, he didn't get into that game with the Kansas City Chiefs. For the next two contests, the Cowboys deactivated him again, meaning he had gone through half the season with no chance to play.

That's when that unusual request came. He asked the Cowboys if they would let him play on special teams. They made that adjustment, and Chad Hennings had his foot in the door. Before the year was out, he had played in all eight remaining regular season games, and he made three playoff games.

Between that year and the 1996 Super Bowl, Hennings improved with each season. He played in thirteen games in 1993, and has played regularly since. In 1994, he recorded 25 tackles and 7½ sacks to serve notice that he was one of the top defenders on one of the top teams in the NFL.

It's been a story of perseverance and dedication for Chad Hennings as he has taken on and conquered new missions in life. Listening to his parents' wise advice guided him on the long road from Elberon, Iowa, to Dallas, by way of the Air Force Academy and the Persian Gulf War. Listening to the spiritual help of a military chaplain directed him to a strong, vibrant faith through trusting in Jesus Christ.

And now as the possessor of three Super Bowl rings, he continues to seek new challenges, new missions. Together with his wife, Tammy, a native Coloradan whom he met while at the Academy, their first mission is to nurture their son, Chase, in a way that pleases God. "We're trying to raise Chase in the light of God's Word."

To accomplish that, the Henningses depend a great deal on small-group Bible studies. Tammy and Chad both participate in Bible Study Fellowship groups, Chad attends the Cowboys' chapel program under the leadership of John Weber, and they have their own devotional times each morning.

Another mission that has attracted Hennings's attention has been the platform available to all pro athletes: to encourage children and adults. Through the Fellowship of Christian Athletes, Athletes in Action, and "any church group that will have me," Chad shares his faith.

"Our country is hurting right now," he says. "We're wanting

morals, we're wanting Christianity back in our schools. We're wanting Christianity back in the mainstream of life. And I've got to do my part to help that along. I think the secret of it all is to give the gospel to our youth. And to be a godly role model to them."

Taking the lead from an opponent in the NFL who is also a Christian brother, Ken Ruettgers of the Green Bay Packers, Hennings has put many of his ideas about commitment in a book. Ruettgers wrote *The Home Field Advantage* in 1995 to express his views on role models, and Hennings's book came off the press as the 1996 season unfolded. It's part of his mission to help young people learn some of the important lessons his parents and his faith have taught him.

The idea of mission is so important to Chad Hennings that he has done something that more people should do. He has developed his own personal missions statement. It is based on Psalm 90:12, which says, "Teach us to number our days aright, that we may gain a heart of wisdom."

From that verse, Hennings has developed a statement that reminds him "to take advantage of every opportunity for God's glory and live today to the fullest."

Even for someone who has been named an All-American, has won a state championship, was selected to the Air Force Academy, was drafted in the NFL, flew a mission of mercy to a needy people in wartime, and won multiple Super Bowl rings, that is perhaps the best mission statement possible.

Q & A WITH CHAD HENNINGS

Q: *What is a typical message you bring when you speak?*
Chad: I talk about trying to maintain a balance. You're committed to your job, and of course, you're committed to your family, but don't let your job overtake your commitment to your family. That comes first.

Picture a cross. There are four points in the cross. It's like the physical aspect and mental aspect of your job and your family, and in the middle is Jesus Christ. He's the One who keeps the balance together. He doesn't let any of those four overtake the others. Christ is like the glue.
Q: *How would you summarize your time flying over Iraq in the war?*
Chad: I call it my Vietnam. Here we're trying to save the Kurdish people, who the Iraqis were trying to commit genocide on. The Turks are

dropping bombs on them, while we were flying overhead trying to save them. So, it was kind of frustrating.

Q: *Is there a downside to playing in the NFL?*
Chad: In training camp we have to be away from our families for six weeks, which is tough. And even after that, we spend a lot of hours in the weight room. Once the season starts, we basically have one day a week off and we usually work out that day. Now I have the opportunity to take my son in with me, so it's not that bad.

Also, if you're one of the high-profile players or if you live in Dallas, where people are fanatical about their team, anywhere you go, people say, "Hey, how you doing?" Or they come up to you while you're eating dinner in a restaurant or what have you and ask for your autograph.

Your time is not yours. I understand it. It's part of the job, so it's not that bad, but when you want to have a quiet evening out with your wife, it can't be done.

Q: *What advice do you have for fathers?*
Chad: Be humble in your heart. Be dedicated and obedient to the Lord, and He will provide. That's tough to take sometimes. To be able to walk blindly in faith, and to be able to just accept that and realize that you can't do it on your own. There are going to be financial burdens. There are going to be external burdens of this world that are going to be thrust on you, but if you keep that in perspective, it's going to make things a lot easier.

Curtis Martin
Running Wild

VITAL STATISTICS

Born May 1, 1973, in Pittsburgh, Pennsylvania
5 feet 11, 203 pounds
College: University of Pittsburgh
Position: Running Back
1996 team: New England Patriots

CAREER HIGHLIGHTS
- Played in the Pro Bowl as a rookie, scoring one touchdown (1996)
- Named 1995 NFL Rookie of the Year
- Led AFC in total yards (1995)
- Received Honorable Mention, college All-American (1993)
- Named to college All-American second team as a freshman (1991)

WARMING UP

He ended the regular season by rushing for more than 100 yards in each of the final five games; for the entire season he exceeded the century mark in nine games. If that seems like a lot for a rookie, it is. He accumulated 1,487 rushing yards, the fourth highest ever for an NFL rookie, trailing only Eric Dickerson, Ottis Anderson, and George Rogers. Clearly Curtis Martin was running wild.

Having passed the biggest test of his athletic ability in his life, the next question for anyone in Curtis Martin's shoes would be: Now how are you going to handle it? Will you forget your heritage and flaunt the newfound fame and money, becoming a caricature of yourself?

Fortunately, Curtis Martin, the mature rookie, did not succumb.

Curtis Martin

t doesn't matter if you're a rabid pro football fan who had never heard of him before the 1995 season, when he ran through defenses with one of the most remarkable rookie performances ever. It doesn't matter if you aren't a New England Patriots fan. It doesn't matter if you aren't even a football fan.

Once you get to know him, you've got to love Curtis Martin.

The stories that surround the life of this strong, stocky football player are already nearing legendary proportions. They are stories of personal strength, overcoming tragedies, and bravely facing what no one should have to endure. And they are stories of goodwill, friendship, and heartfelt love.

Let's start with a couple of stories from his rookie year—a rookie year in which he went from being the seventy-fourth player picked in the draft to the top rookie in the league. In a year that featured such high-priced and highly sought-after running backs as Ki-Jana Carter and Rashaan Salaam, it was Curtis Martin who by the season's end was sneaking up into the top echelon of NFL runners, nipping at the talented heels of Barry Sanders and Emmitt Smith.

But the stories that accompany Martin's entrance into pro football are the kinds of stories that men set their little boys down to tell.

One story has to do with Martin and a nine-year-old Massachusetts boy. Now, everybody who knows anything about rich professional athletes knows that they've heard all the requests that naive little boys can make, and they've found slick answers to turn all of them down.

Adults may know that, but not little boys. Martin, who is small by NFL standards at 5 feet 11, still must have towered over this boy who approached him after a Patriots game. The youngster innocently and eagerly walked up to and invited him to his birthday party.

"Can you come?"

Right, kid. And why not ask the President to stop by for burgers while you're at it!

Surely Curtis Martin had something better to do. After all, there are the constant requests for interviews, the endorsements, the rigid practice schedule, the autographing sessions, and a hundred other things athletes have to do. Surely the big-shot pro could fast-talk his way out of this one.

Surely not.

When it came time for the birthday party, who showed up but Curtis Martin. Not followed by a phalanx of reporters and not forced into it by an overeager agent looking for good publicity. Just Curtis Martin and his smile. He ate the cake. He signed the autographs. He even sang the song.

Just Curtis and the guys.

Right away you sense that there is something refreshing and intriguing about this football player. His accessibility contrasts with the typical arm's-length attitude of so many athletes. It makes you wonder why—why is Curtis Martin so different?

You might also wonder this when you consider a second incident that occurred during Martin's initial run through the NFL. Ruben Brown was a rookie offensive guard for the Buffalo Bills in 1995. Curtis Martin, of course, was a rookie running back for the Pats. On October 23, their paths crossed during a Monday Night Football contest.

It was a reunion of sorts. They had spent a lot of time sharing the turf as teammates at the University of Pittsburgh. Beyond that, they were friends. And on this Monday night in October, Brown did what comes so naturally for friends who play games. When Martin ran the ball in for a touchdown, Brown celebrated on the sidelines.

Unfortunately, when he jumped for joy as Martin scurried across the goal line, Brown was standing on the Bills' sideline with his new teammates. Brown's a big guy, but perhaps not big enough to keep from incurring the wrath of about fifty other gridiron giants who don't take kindly to one of their mates playing cheerleader for the other team.

Later Brown told reporters, "When he ran in the touchdown against us, I was kind of cheering a little bit. But I knew what he went through. . . . It felt good to see him score a touchdown."

Curtis Martin inspires that kind of loyalty. Those who know what Martin has endured in his life can hardly help but be "cheering a little bit" every time he succeeds on the football field. After all, the greatest stories about the NFL's 1995 Rookie of the Year are the stories that detail his life before he burst onto the pro football scene.

Curtis Martin is at once the most unlikely and the most likely person to be wearing an NFL uniform. Unlikely in the sense that his chances of even growing up to be old enough to play in an adult league could have been described as minimal as a kid growing up in Pittsburgh. Likely in the sense that his skill was clearly evident the first time he played high school football.

The streets in the neighborhood where Curtis Martin grew up were mean indeed. The only child of a single mom, Curtis readily admits that he "grew up in a part of Pittsburgh that people would consider one of the harder parts of town."

His mom worked three jobs just to provide a roof for the two of them. And when she was gone to work, Curtis stayed either with a neighboring family, the Stantons, or with his grandmother. "A few of my mother's friends would watch me sometimes," he explains. "Many times when I was younger, I would come home by myself. I wasn't too scared to stay in the house by myself."

When Martin was just nine years old, the streets claimed his grandmother. One day when Curtis's mom went to check on her mother, she discovered her body with a knife sticking out of her chest. "Someone who knew my grandmother robbed her and stabbed her to death," Martin says.

So how does an elementary school kid respond to such senseless tragedy? For some, it could be devastating, paralyzing, hardening. By now, young Curtis Martin had already seen enough sadness. How would this new, jarring incident affect him? He seemed to handle it with a maturity that cannot be measured in years.

"It had an impact on me," he recalls. "I believe that I've always been the type not to let things get me down. . . . I remember telling my mother, 'You can't let this get you down. You've got to be strong and live and take care of me.' I was so young, but that was like something that encouraged her not to allow that to affect her in a way that would have made her go crazy."

Nine years old, giving counsel to his mother about how to handle the grief over her mother's murder! Already there was a depth to Curtis Martin that would help carry him through future trials.

Looking back on this tragedy, Martin can see now how important his response was, not just to his mom but to his own well-being in the next nine years of his life. "Me and my grandmother were just as close as me and my mother. I spent a lot of time with her. I see how being able to go through her death was something that has made me strong in life. By my dealing with that, it was so much easier for me to deal with so many other things."

Life was not going to get any easier for Martin as he grew into his teenage years. "Because of the part of town where I was from, I experienced a lot of my friends being killed. A lot of people were put in jail for a long period of time. A lot of people were crippled. One of my friends was crippled from being shot. I myself had experienced a lot of times that I know was so close that I almost got killed—just being in the wrong place at the wrong time. You would just be out having fun and the bullets would just start flying."

Young Curtis had avoided bullets on Pittsburgh's wild streets, and you might assume that like other young people in the inner city's wild streets that he found a safe haven from it all in sports. A haven that would launch him into the NFL.

Not true. For most of his high school years, football was not that haven. Although Martin did play sports while he was growing up, especially baseball, he did not play high school football for the first three years.

Football is a game of discipline, led by men who demand it and teach it. For Martin, this kind of situation had little appeal. He was not interested in the rigid life of an athlete. "I was just really into running around the streets and hanging out. I was like, *Oh, man, I don't have time to be rolling around on the ground, doing push-ups for some guy.* That's how I looked at it.

"At the same time, I knew I had fun when I did play." It certainly seemed like more fun than some of those summers on the streets of Pittsburgh. He remembers one summer when "twenty-something people or friends or relatives had gotten killed."

That's when Curtis's mother made the second-sport decision for him. She had listened to her little boy offer his wise, childlike advice when he was just nine. Now she was ready to offer her own brand of take-it-or-leave-it wisdom.

"My mother's attitude was, 'You need to do something just to stay out of the way!'" She didn't want her boy to be the next youngster catching a stray bullet.

At about the same time, Mark Witgarner, Martin's gym teacher at Allderdice High School, offered his own assessment of Curtis's situation. He told the hangin' out, soon-to-be senior, "I know that if you were to play football, you could earn a scholarship to college."

Fortunately, Martin had begun to do some assessing of his own, and he realized that his own prospects did not look good. "I saw what happens when you just stay around this area or just stay around and hang out and don't do anything after you get out of high school. I saw a lot of people with a lot of talent who, later on, were killed or wasted their lives.

"I said to myself, *I know it's for me to go to college.* I just believed in my heart."

So when the 1990 football season began at Allderdice High, the team had a brand-new running back. A first-year kid, just trying out the varsity sport: a senior named Curtis Martin.

His performance didn't suggest a first-year runner. Four times in his first and last season of high school ball, Martin rushed for 200-plus yards in a game. For the year, he ground out 1,705 yards, averaging 7.4 yards a carry. Along the way, he carried the ball across the goal line 20 times. He was running wild. No defense could tame him.

The honors rolled in: All-State, City League Player of the Year, and Most Valuable Player of the Maryland-Pennsylvania "Big 33" All-Star Game.

Yet even during this triumphant senior year—this coming-out year as a football player for Curtis Martin—tragedy still chased him like a crazed inside linebacker. "One of my best friends got shot in the chest my senior year of high school," Martin recalls. "They used to compare us. We used to push each other to do well. Right after the season, he got killed."

Martin somehow had survived the streets long enough to get a chance at the gridiron. But he wondered why he had avoided the violence, evading the seemingly inevitable tragic ending that felled so many of his friends? The answer, he says, began to show itself while he was in high school. "It took me until going into my junior year to recognize that everything that happens isn't luck. It's because, I believe in my heart, God was protecting me."

Yet while he was in high school, Martin had neither the knowledge nor the inclination to take action on this inkling that Someone had a special hand of protection on him. He was not a churchgoer. And there was no reason to think that he ever would become one.

After Martin's outstanding senior year of high school he got the big chance his high school coach had promised him: a football scholarship. He would receive a college education at the University of Pittsburgh and become a running back for the Panthers.

For a kid who had sneaked out of the 'hood with his life, it might seem a little risky to go to school so close to the action. It might even seem wise to get as far out of town as possible and never look back. That's not the kind of thinking that marked Curtis Martin's life when he was eighteen years old. He wanted to "stay close to home" near his mother. But that wasn't the main reason he stayed in Pittsburgh. "I just felt that this is where I'm supposed to be."

It didn't take long for Pitt fans to agree.

One game tells it all. In a nationally televised nonconference game against Minnesota, Martin introduced himself to America by rushing for 170 yards on 18 carries, including a 36-yard touchdown scamper. To round out his game, he caught 5 passes for another 42 yards. The folks at ABC were so impressed they named Martin the Chevrolet Player of the Game.

Right out of the blocks this kid, who just about a year earlier had decided he might want to play a little football, was nationally known. Yet there was no rip-off-the-helmet, look-at-me razzmatazz coming from Martin. Of his reaction to his sudden fame as a freshman, Martin says no more than, "It just seems that it was never in me to be the big-shot attitude type of guy. God has blessed me with a certain humbleness." No more needed to be said.

Martin finished his initial college season with 556 yards on 114 carries, a mark that was good enough to earn him second-team honors on the *Football News* freshman All-American team. Not that it really made a lot of difference to Curtis.

After a rather lackluster sophomore year in which he started only four games for the Panthers and suffered numerous niggling injuries, Martin broke through in a big way in his third year at Pitt. He crossed the 1,000-yard threshold with 75 yards to spare on his way to being named an honorable mention All-American. The run that put him over that plateau was a spectacular 80-yard trek in the season finale. His score clinched the Panthers' victory in that game with Temple. In addition to that great performance, he ran roughshod over Syracuse for 206 yards in mid-October.

With his senior year still on the horizon, Martin's football career looked limitless. Preseason All-American teams listed his name, and the Big East Conference appeared to be a Curtis Martin showcase. On September 3, those expectations began to be realized. Against the storied Texas Longhorns, Martin rustled up a 251-yard afternoon, averaging 7.3 yards per carry. It must have felt like high school all over again, as he nearly matched his 7.4 yards a carry average from his senior year at Allderdice.

Next up was Ohio University. Against the Bobcats, Martin had picked up 31 yards as the nonconference game plowed into the second quarter.

Then the unthinkable happened. He suffered a sprained ankle. For someone who has been through so much, a sprained ankle doesn't sound like much. But this injury was lethal to his college career. Unable to fully rehab the ankle, Martin never carried the ball again for the Pitt Panthers. He had come so far, and it ended with a rolled ankle.

Yet something had happened to Martin about a year earlier that had him prepared for such an unfortunate eventuality. His tough spirit, built up over time through his tough circumstances, may have enabled him to endure the hardship of losing most of his senior season, but he needed more.

He needed faith.

"My freshman and sophomore years," he explains, "God wasn't even on my mind."

But after his sophomore year at Pitt, he began to reflect on his years running wild in the city and how fortunate he was to have not only survived but to have the opportunity to get a college education. It all began to click for him

I need to get my life together, he told himself. He realized his life hadn't changed one bit from high school. *I don't want to be like this the rest of my life.*

Staying in his hometown to play college ball, Martin realized he had not left "all the things that were going on in Pittsburgh. I started wondering if I was going to end up dead, or be just another statistic. One who they say, 'Well, he could have done good. He could have played in the NFL. He could have been successful. But he got killed.' I saw that happening even more so when I was in college with a lot of my friends.

"It got to the point that I was worried about going out of the house. My mother was worried about me—even getting out of the car. I had been living like this too long with that frame of mind."

He soon realized that his avoiding harm's way was not luck but God's protection. "All the times I could have gotten hurt or killed even, I just always came up without a scratch on me. I knew that there was more to it than good luck.

"I realized that God had something special planned for me. . . . I began to just feel, *I've got to thank Him and show Him that I'm grateful.* Back then my thought was, *I'll just start going to church.* I didn't know what it would lead to."

So, after his sophomore year, Martin started going to church in the summer. The streets were still calling, and Martin looked for a safe place to avoid their call. There he heard the gospel of Jesus Christ. He found out that the only safe place on earth is in Jesus. "It became something that I wanted to be committed to. I wanted to serve God, so I got saved. I accepted Christ as my Lord and Savior.

"I knew there was a space that only God could fill. When I went to God, it was with the attitude, *I'm tired of trying to live my life. I just pray that You guide me no matter what I do. And no matter what it takes, show me what I'm supposed to be doing in life.* I prayed that He would show me what His purpose was in my life."

His faith bolstered him during a long, hard senior season, one in which NFL dreams wavered like a flickering flame on a windy night. The slow healing ankle turned Martin's newest concerns from whether he'd get into trouble to whether he'd get into the NFL. But his previous performances were enough to impress more than one pro scout. Among those showing interest were the powerful Dallas Cowboys.

On draft day, the Cowboys were at his house, perhaps looking a bit like a Publishers' Clearinghouse prize squad, offering a contract filled with big numbers. "They told me they were going to pick me," Martin recalls. "They expected to get me first or second."

But they didn't. Sometime during the proceedings, the Cowboys bowed out, leaving the field open. Finally, in the third round, using a pick obtained from the Philadelphia Eagles, the New England Patriots nabbed Martin.

"I was expecting to go higher just because of what the coaches had told me. At the same time, it wasn't any big deal to me. The only difference was the money, and that wasn't any big difference for me. It was just that I would be grateful that I was just playing—that they were even drafting me, because I just played that one game my senior year."

You might want to read that paragraph again, because you certainly won't see many quotes like that floating around the NFL, the NBA, MLB, the NHL, or any other league with three letters in it.

And he's not kidding. To Curtis Martin, gratefulness comes before everything else.

He was even grateful that the Cowboys went home without his name on their contract. And for anyone who might have to face the prospect of being a replacement player for Emmitt Smith, it is understandable that Curtis declares, "I'm glad that I went to New England."

So's New England. Martin was one of the few lights shining through the fog. After a promising second year, quarterback Drew Bledsoe had an especially disappointing year, ending as the lowest ranking passer in the AFC. For coach Bill Parcells, it was the kind of troubling year that leaves a coach answering more questions about where he's planning to coach next year than what he's coaching this year.

But for Martin, not much went wrong. From game one, he let the whole nation know that he was back. He picked up where he had left off in the second game of his senior year.

Look at what he did in his rookie year:

September 3: 102 yards, a record for Patriot rookies in their first game
October 23: 127 yards on 36 carries

November 5: 170 yards
November 12: 142 yards against Miami, becoming the first player
in 20 games to gain more than 100 yards against Miami
November 26: 148 yards against Buffalo
December 3: 112 yards against New Orleans
December 10: 148 yards against the New York Jets
December 16: 120 yards against Pittsburgh
December 23: 102 yards against Indianapolis

Martin had ended the regular season by rushing for more than 100 yards in each of the final five games; for the entire season he had exceeded the century mark in nine games. If that seems like a lot for a rookie, it is. He accumulated 1,487 rushing yards, the fourth highest ever for an NFL rookie, trailing only Eric Dickerson, Ottis Anderson, and George Rogers.

Clearly Curtis Martin was running wild. He had set a new Patriots' mark for rushing yardage in one season. He had led the AFC in rushing as well as total yardage (1,748).

Besides earning Martin the Rookie of the Year Award, these stats also put him in the Pro Bowl as the only rookie. Along with Chris Warren of Seattle and Marshall Faulk of Indianapolis, Martin was selected to run the ball for the AFC. But it was as a receiver that he shone most brightly in the Hawaii sun at the game. He and quarterback Jim Harbaugh of the Colts hooked up for a 17-yard touchdown that kept the game close for the AFC.

Having passed the biggest test of his athletic ability in his life, the next question for anyone in Curtis Martin's shoes would be: Now how are you going to handle it? Will you forget your heritage and flaunt the newfound fame and money, becoming a caricature of yourself?

It happens so often in sports we can barely keep track. Fortunately, this mature rookie did not succumb. Instead, his gratitude overruled pride.

"Every time something else happens," he says, "it's like, 'Wow, God. I just appreciate this. I know You know my heart, and I just want to tell You how much I appreciate what You've done for me.'"

Curtis Martin hasn't abandoned the neighborhood where he grew up. His mom still works in the area, and Curtis still returns. But he goes with a purpose far different from the one he had as a high school junior who was too busy working the streets to work on the football field.

"I don't go back just to hang out. Most of the bad things that happen happen at a party. Being a Christian teaches me how I don't have to watch my every step. I don't put myself in dangerous situations. You learn to put yourself in better positions. Now everyone knows that I'm a Christian.

"Now they see the way I live my life. Ninety-nine percent of the people who know me can see the drastic, drastic change in my life from then to now.

"Besides football and fame and all that, it's the inner change. It's more or less a witness to them, and it makes them want to strive for that. I am so grateful for that. When I go to my neighborhood, I can talk to some of the people who are possibly murderers or big drug people. The ones that I really get to spend a lot of time with really change their whole lives around. And I'm grateful just to be able to see that. It's a wonderful feeling. It's almost like being able to see myself change from how I used to be, from that sinful type of life.

"I believe that one thing God has taught me is that I know the meaning of purpose. I don't think God will reveal my purpose to me and say, 'This is what you have to do for the rest of your life.' I believe He gives you a concept and a vision, but I believe He leads you and guides you if you're abiding in Him. I think that if you understand your purpose in life, you can never fail. If you fall down, you can get back up and go again.

"I believe God has given me a good grasp of what my purpose is. I know it involves touching lives and His being able to use me to touch other people's lives."

Curtis Martin may still run wild, but he also runs with a purpose. How can you not like a guy like that?

Q & A WITH CURTIS MARTIN

Q: *Your first year in the NFL was full of great events. What was the highlight of 1995?*

Curtis: Playing against Pittsburgh. The Pro Bowl and everything were definitely honors, but to come home and play against the Steelers was just one of those things where I was most excited. Just about everyone I know was either there or watching.

Q: *You've been very open about your faith in interviews. Have you received any negative reaction?*

Curtis: No, there's really been no negative reaction. I believe there's a time or place to talk about faith. I don't think that every time a reporter asks a question, I have to talk about God. When the time is right, I'll talk about it. When they ask me about football, we'll talk about football.

A lot of people don't have the same effect because a lot of reporters won't even come and talk to them. The writers know all they'll talk about is God, and they don't want to talk about it.

If my teammates ask me about faith, I'm more than willing to talk about it with them. But when we're around, they look at me as one of the guys. They feel comfortable. They don't feel like Curt is so holy he can't talk regular.

Q: *What do you do to stay sharp spiritually?*

Curtis: Besides living according to God, I study a lot. I might study the Bible and write different things about the Scriptures. I have Bible studies where some of the teammates come. A lot of things like that. That's not just during the season, but all year.

I like to read a Bible passage and then write down different things about it. Like: "Your reputation is who others say you are, but your character is who you really are." I write these on the board in the locker room.

During the season, I think my life should be lived so that when a trial comes, I don't have to start studying extra. I want to live my life in a state of readiness so that I don't have to start studying or going to church when I know something is about to go wrong.

Q: *What is your favorite Scripture passage?*
Curtis: When I got to New England, my number got switched from 29 to 28 and I was talking to my pastor and as soon as I said that, he said, "Deuteronomy 28." Ever since then, I've loved verses 1–14, which tell us the blessings for obedience.

Q: *What kind of people-helping ministries do you enjoy most?*
Curtis: I just came from South Hills, way out in the suburbs of Pittsburgh. I've hardly been out there in my life. For me, wherever I can be used, I'm willing to go. It doesn't have to be in my neighborhood. Sometimes I'll just go on my own to the basketball games and sit with the kids.

The other day, I went to the Y and just had fun with the kids. I just laugh with them and maybe take a couple of kids out to eat. Just having fun with them. I feel that my ministry doesn't have to be limited to anything. It doesn't have to be planned.

I believe I've gotten into a relationship with God where it doesn't surprise me when He uses me. . . . I'm not saying that I'm so good, it's just that God is using me. That doesn't surprise me. He's God. It just makes my heart grow more and more. I tell Him, "You don't have to be using me," but He's choosing me.